To The Work! To The Work!
Exhortations to Christians

Dwight L. Moody

To The Work! To The Work! Exhortations to Christians

Copyright © 2020 Bibliotech Press
All rights reserved

The present edition is a reproduction of previous publication of this classic work. Minor typographical errors may have been corrected without note, however, for an authentic reading experience the spelling, punctuation, and capitalization have been retained from the original text.

ISBN: 978-1-64799-023-7

CONTENTS

CHAPTER I	"TAKE YE AWAY THE STONE"	1
CHAPTER II	LOVE, THE MOTIVE POWER FOR SERVICE ………………………....	14
CHAPTER III	FAITH AND COURAGE ………………..	28
CHAPTER IV	FAITH REWARDED ……………………..	42
CHAPTER V	ENTHUSIASM ……………………………..	49
CHAPTER VI	THE POWER OF LITTLE THINGS ………..	60
CHAPTER VII	"SHE HATH DONE WHAT SHE COULD"	76
CHAPTER VIII	"WHO IS MY NEIGHBOR?" …………….....	88
CHAPTER IX	"YE ARE THE LIGHT OF THE WORLD" ...	101

CHAPTER I

TAKE YE AWAY THE STONE

In the gospel by John we read that at the tomb of Lazarus our Lord said to His disciples, "Take ye away the stone." Before the act of raising Lazarus could be performed, the disciples had their part to do. Christ could have removed the stone with a word. It would have been very easy for Him to have commanded it to roll away, and it would have obeyed His voice, as the dead Lazarus did when He called him back to life. But the Lord would have His children learn this lesson: that they have something to do towards raising the spiritually dead. The disciples had not only to take away the stone, but after Christ had raised Lazarus they had to "loose and let him go."

It is a question if any man on the face of the earth has ever been converted, without God using some human instrument, in some way. God could easily convert men without us; but that is not His way.

The stone I want to speak about to-day, that must be rolled away before any great work of God can be brought about, is the miserable stone of prejudice. Many people have a great prejudice against revivals; they hate the very word. I am sorry to say that this feeling is not confined to ungodly or careless people; there are not a few Christians who seem to cherish a strong dislike both to the word "Revival" and to the thing itself.

What does "Revival" mean? It simply means a recalling from obscurity—a finding some hidden treasure and bringing it back to the light. I think every one of us must acknowledge that we are living in a time of need. I doubt if there is a family in the world that has not some relative whom they would like to see brought into the fold of God, and who needs salvation.

Men are anxious for a revival in business. I am told that there is a widespread and general stagnation in business. People are very anxious that there should be a revival of trade this winter. There a great revival in politics just now. In all departments of life you find that men are very anxious for a revival in the things that concern them most.

If this is legitimate—and I do not say but it is perfectly right in its place—should not every child of God be praying for and desiring a revival of godliness in the world at the present time. Do we not need a revival of downright honesty, of truthfulness, of uprightness, and of temperance? Are there not many who have become alienated from the Church of God and from the house of the Lord, who are forming an attachment to the saloon? Are not our sons being drawn away by hundreds and thousands, so that while you often find the churches empty, the liquor shops are crowded every Sabbath afternoon and evening. I am sure the saloon-keepers are glad if they can have a revival in their business; they do not object to sell more whisky and beer. Then surely every true Christian ought to desire that men who are in danger of perishing eternally should be saved and rescued.

Some people seem to think that "Revivals" are a modern invention—that they have only been known within the last few years. But they are nothing new. If there is not Scriptural authority for revivals, then I cannot understand my Bible.

For the first 2,000 years of the world's history they had no revival that we know of; probably, if they had, there would have been no Flood. The first real awakening, of which we read in the Old Testament, was when Moses was sent down to Egypt to bring his brethren out of the house of bondage. When Moses went down to Goshen, there must have been a great commotion there; many things were done out of the usual order. When three millions of Hebrews were put behind the Blood of the Slain Lamb, that was nothing but God reviving His work among them.

Under Joshua there was a great revival; and again under the Judges. God was constantly reviving the Jewish nation in those olden times. Samuel brought the people to Mizpah, and told them to put away their strange gods. Then the Israelites went out and defeated the Philistines, so that they never came back in his day. Dr. Bonar says it may be that David and Jonathan were converted under that revival in the time of Samuel.

What was it but a great revival in the days of Elijah? The people had turned away to idolatry, and the prophet summoned them to Mount Carmel. As the multitude stood there on the mountain, God answered by fire; the people fell on their faces and cried, "The Lord, He is the God." That was the nation turning back to God. No doubt there were men talking against the work, and saying it would not last. That is the cry of many to-day, and has been the cry for 4,000 years. Some old Carmelite very probably said in the days of Elijah: "This will not be permanent." So there are not a few in these days shaking their wise heads and saying the work will not last.

When we come to New Testament times, we have the wonderful revival under John the Baptist. Was there ever a man who accomplished so much in a few months, except the Master Himself? The preaching of John was like the breath of spring after a long and dreary winter. For 400 long years there had been no prophet, and darkness had settled down on the nation. John's advent was like the flashing of a brilliant meteor that heralded the coming day. It was not in the temple or in any synagogue that he preached, but on the banks of the Jordan. Men, women, and children flocked to hear him. Almost any one can get an audience in a crowded city, but this was away out in the desert. No doubt there was great excitement. I suppose the towns and villages were nearly depopulated, as they flocked out to hear the preaching of John.

People are so afraid of excitement. When I went over to England in 1867, I was asked to go and preach at the Derby race-course. I saw more excitement there in one day than I have seen at all the religious meetings I ever attended in my life put together. And yet I heard no one complaining of too much excitement. I heard of a minister, not long ago, who was present at a public dance till after five o'clock in the morning. The next Sabbath he preached against the excitement of revivals—the late hours, and so on. Very consistent kind of reasoning, was it not?

Then look at Pentecost. The apostles preached, and you know what the result was. I suppose the worldly men of that day said it would all die away. Although they brought about the martyrdom of Stephen and of James, other men rose up to take possession of the field. From the very place where Stephen was slain, Saul took up the work, and it has been going on ever since.

There are many professed Christians who are all the time finding fault and criticising. They criticise the preaching, or the singing. The prayers will be either too long or too short, too loud, or not loud enough. They will find fault with the reading of the Word of God, or will say it was not the right portion. They will criticise the preacher. "I do not like his style," they say. If you doubt what I say, listen to the people as they go out of a revival meeting, or any other religious gathering.

"What did you think of the preacher?" says one. "Well, I must confess I was disappointed. I did not like his manner. He was not graceful in his actions." Another will say: "He was not logical; I like logic." Or another: "He did not preach enough about repentance." If a preacher does not go over every doctrine in every sermon people begin to find fault. They say: "There was too much repentance, and no Gospel; or, it was all Gospel, and no repentance." "He spoke a great deal abort justification, but he said nothing about sanctification." So if a man does not go right through the Bible, from Genesis to Revelation, in one sermon, they at once proceed to criticise and find fault.

"The fact is," says some one of this class, "the man did not touch my heart at all." Some one else will say, "He was all heart and no head. I like a man to preach to my intellect." Or, "He appeals too much to the will; he does not give enough prominence to the doctrine of election." Or, again, "There is no backbone in his preaching; he does not lay sufficient stress on doctrine." Or, "He is not eloquent;" and so on, and so on.

You may find hundreds of such fault-finders among professed Christians; but all their criticism will not lead one solitary soul to Christ. I never preached a sermon yet that I could not pick to pieces and find fault with. I feel that Jesus Christ ought to have a far better representative than I am. But I have lived long enough to discover that there is nothing perfect in this world. If you are to wait until you can find a perfect preacher, or perfect meetings, I am afraid you will have to wait till the millennium arrives. What we want is to be looking right up to Him. Let us get done with fault-finding. When I hear people talk in the way I have described, I say to them, "Come and do better yourself. Step up here and try what you can do." My friends, it is so easy to find fault; it takes neither brains nor heart.

Some years ago, a pastor of a little Church in a small town became exceedingly discouraged, and brooded over his trials to such an extent that he became an inveterate grumbler. He found fault with his brethren because he imagined they did not treat him well. A brother minister was invited to assist him a few days in a special service. At the close of the Sabbath morning service our unhappy brother invited the minister to his house to dinner. While they were waiting alone in the parlor, he began his doleful story by saying: "My brother, you have no idea of my troubles; and one of the greatest is, my brethren in the Church treat me very badly." The other propounded the following questions:

"Did they ever spit in your face?"

"No; they haven't come to that."

"Did they ever smite you?" "No."

"Did they ever crown you with thorns?"

This last question he could not answer, but bowed his head thoughtfully. His brother replied: "Your Master and mine was thus treated, and all His disciples fled and left Him in the hands of the wicked. Yet He opened not His mouth." The effect of this conversation was wonderful. Both ministers bowed in prayer and earnestly sought to possess the mind which was in Christ Jesus. During the ten days' meetings the discontented pastor became wonderfully changed. He labored and prayed with his friend, and many souls were brought to Christ. Some weeks after, a deacon of the church wrote and said: "Your late visit and conversation with our pastor have had a wonderful influence for good. We never hear him complain now, and he labors more prayerfully and zealously." Another charge brought against revivals is that they are out of the regular order of things. Well, there is no doubt about that. But that does not prove that they are wrong. Eldad and Medad were out of the regular succession. Joshua wanted Moses to rebuke them. Instead of that he said: "Would God that all the Lord's people were prophets." Elijah and Elisha did not belong to the regular school of prophets, yet they exercised a mighty influence for good in their day. John the Baptist was not in the regular line. He got his theological training out in the desert. Jesus Christ Himself was out of the recognized order. When Philip told Nathaniel that he had found the Messiah, he said to him: "Can there any good thing come out of Nazareth?"

As we read the history of the past few centuries we find that God has frequently taken up those who were, so to speak, out of the regular line. Martin Luther had to break through the regular order of things in his day before he brought about the mighty Reformation. There are now some sixty millions of people who adhere to the Lutheran Church. Wesley and Whitefield were not exactly in the regular line, but see what a mighty work they accomplished!

My friends, when God works many things will be done "out of the regular order." It seems to me that will be a good thing. There are a few who cannot be reached, apparently, through the regular channels, who will come to meetings like these out of the usual routine. We have got our churches, it is true, but we want to make an effort to reach the outlying masses who will not go to them. Many will come in to these meetings simply because they are to be held only for a few days. And so, if they are to come at all, they must come to a decision about it quickly. Others come out of idle curiosity, or a desire to know what is going on. And often at the first meeting something that is spoken or that is sung will touch them. They have come under the sound of the Gospel; probably they will become real Christians and useful members of society. You will sometimes hear people say, "We have our churches; if men will not come to them, let them keep out." That was not the spirit of the Master. When our Civil War broke out we had a very small standing army. Government asked for volunteers to enlist. Several hundreds of thousands of men came forward and joined the ranks of the regular army. There was plenty for every man to do. These volunteers were not so well trained and drilled as the older solders, but we could use the irregulars as well as the regulars. Many of the former soon became efficient soldiers, and these volunteers did great service in the cause of the nation. If the outlying masses of the people are to be reached we must have the regulars and the irregulars both.

I remember hearing of a Sunday-school in our country where the teacher had got into ruts. A young man was placed in charge as Superintendent, and he wanted to re-arrange the seats. Some of the older members said the seats had been in their present position for so many years, that they could not be moved! There is a good deal of that kind of spirit nowadays. It seems to me that if one method is not successful we ought to give it up and try some other plan that may be more likely to succeed. If the people will not come to the "regular means of grace," let us adopt some means that will reach them and win them.

Do not let us be finding fault because things are not done exactly as they have been done in the past, and as we think they ought to be done. I am sick and tired of those who are constantly complaining. Let us pay no heed to them, but let us go forward with the work that God has given us to do.

Another very serious charge is brought against revivals. They say the work will not last. As I have said there were doubtless many at the day of Pentecost who said that. And when Stephen was stoned to death, James beheaded, and finally all the apostles put to death, no doubt they said that Pentecost was a stupendous failure. But was it a failure? Are not the fruits of that revival at Pentecost to be seen even in our time?

In the sight of the world the mission of John the Baptist may have been thought to be a failure when he was beheaded by the command of Herod. But it was not a failure in the sight of heaven. The influence of this wilderness prophet is felt in the Church of God to-day. The world thought Christ's life was a failure as He hung on the Cross and expired. But in the sight of God it was altogether different. God made the wrath of men to praise Him.

I have little sympathy with those pastors who, when God is reviving the Churches, begin to preach against revivals. There is not a denomination in Christendom to-day that has not sprung out of a revival. The Roman Catholics and the Episcopalians both claim to be apostolic in their origin; if they are, they sprang out of the revival at Pentecost. The Methodist body rose out of revivals under John Wesley and George Whitefield. Did not the Lutheran Church come from the great awakening that swept through Germany in the days of Luther? Was not Scotland stirred up through the preaching of John Knox? Where did the Quakers come from if not from the work of God under George Fox? Yet people are so afraid if the regular routine of things is going to be disturbed. Let us pray that God may raise up many who will be used by Him for the reviving of His Church in our day. I think the time has come when we need it.

I remember we went into one place where one of the ministers found that his Church was opposed to his taking part in the meetings. He was told that if he identified himself with the movement he would alienate some of his congregation. He took the Church record and found that four-fifths of the members of the Church had been converted in times of revival, among others the Superintendent of the Sabbath-school, all the officers of the Church, and nearly every active member. The minister went into the Church the following Sabbath and preached a sermon on revivals, reminding them of what had taken place in the history of the congregation. You will find that many who talk against revivals have themselves been converted in such a time.

Not long ago a very able minister preached a sermon against these awakenings; he did not believe in them. Some of his people searched the Church records to see how many during the previous twelve years had been added to the membership on profession of their faith; they found that not a single soul had joined the Church all these years on profession of faith. No wonder the minister of a Church like that preached against revivals!

My experience has been that those who are converted in a time of special religious interest make even stronger Christians than those who were brought into the Church at ordinary times. One young convert helps another, and they get a better start in the Christian life when there are a good many together.

People say the converts sill not hold out. Well, they did not all hold out under the preaching of Jesus Christ. "Many of His disciples went back and walked no more with Him." Paul mourned over the fact that some of those who made profession were walking as the enemies of the Cross of Christ. The Master taught in His wonderful parable that there are various kinds of hearers—those represented by the wayside hearers, the stony ground hearers, the thorny ground hearers, and the good ground hearers; they will remain to the end of time. I have a fruit tree at my home, and every year it has so many blossoms that if they should all produce apples the tree would break down. Nine-tenths, perhaps, of the blossoms will fall off, and yet I have a large number of apples.

So there are many who make a profession of Christianity who fall away. It may be that those who seemed to promise the fairest turn out the worst, and those who did not promise so well turn out best in the end. God must prepare the ground and He must give the increase. I have often said that if I had to convict men of sin I would have given up the work long ago. That is the work of the Holy Ghost. What we have to do is to scatter the good seed of the Word, and expect that God will bless it to the saving of men's souls.

Of course we cannot expect much help from those who are all the time talking against revivals. I believe many young disciples are chilled through by those who condemn these special efforts. If the professed converts sometimes do not hold out, it is not always their own fault.

I was preaching in a certain city some time ago, and a minister said to me: "I hope this work will not turn out like the revival here five years ago. I took one hundred converts into the Church, and, with the exception of one or two, I do not know where they are today." This was discouraging. I mentioned it to another minister in the same city, and I said I would rather give up the work, and go back to business, if the work was not going to last. He said to me: "I took in one hundred converts at the same time, and I can lay my hand on ninety-eight out of the hundred. For five years I have watched them, and only two have fallen away." Then he asked me if his brother minister had told me what took place in his Church after they brought in those young converts. Some of them thought they ought to have a better Church, and they got divided among themselves; so nearly all the members left the Church. If anyone will but engage heartily in this work they will have enough to encourage them.

It is very easy for men to talk against a work like this. But we generally find that such people not only do nothing at all themselves, but they know nothing about that which they are criticising. Surely it is hardly fair to condemn a work that we have not been at the trouble to become personally acquainted with. If, instead of sitting on the platform and simply looking on or criticising, such persons would get down among the people and talk to them about their souls, they would soon find out whether the work was real or not.

I remember hearing of a man who returned from a residence in India. He was out at dinner one day with some friends, and he was asked about Missions; he said he had never seen a native convert all the time he was in India. A missionary who was present did not reply directly to the statement, but he quietly asked the sceptical Englishman if he had seen any tigers in India. The man rubbed his hands, as if the recollection gave him a good deal of pleasure, and said: "Tigers! Yes, I should think so. I have shot a good many of them." Said the missionary, "Well, I was in India for a number of years and never saw a tiger." The fact was that the one had been looking for converts and the other for tigers, and they both found what they looked for.

If we look for converts we shall find them; there is no doubt about that. But the truth is that in almost every case those who talk against revivals know nothing whatever about it from personal contact and experience. Do you suppose that the young converts are going round to your house and knock at the door to tell you they have been converted? If you wish to find out the truth you must go among them in their homes and talk to them.

I hope no one will be afraid of the Inquiry Room. At one of the places where I worked once I found a good many people who hated the very word "Inquiry Room." But I contend that it is a perfectly reasonable thing. When a boy is at school and cannot solve some problem in algebra, he asks help of some one who knows it. Here is the great problem of eternal life that has to be solved by each of us. Why should we not ask those who are more experienced than ourselves to help us if they can. If we have any difficulty we cannot overcome, probably we shall find some Godly man or woman who had the same difficulty twenty years ago; they will be glad to help us, and tell us how they were enabled to surmount it. Do not be afraid therefore to let them help you.

I believe there is not a living soul who has a spiritual difficulty but there is some promise in the Word of God to meet that difficulty. But if you keep your feelings and your troubles all locked up, how are you to be helped? I might stand here and preach to you right on for thirty days and not touch your particular difficulty. But twenty minutes' private conversation may clear away all your doubts and troubles.

There was a lady who worked in the Inquiry Room when we were in the south of London nine years ago. I saw her again a short time ago, and she told me that she had a list of thirty-five cases of those with whom she conversed, and who she thought were truly converted. She has written letters to them and sent them little gifts at Christmas, and she said to me that so far as she could judge not a single one of the thirty-five had wandered away. She has placed her life alongside of theirs all these years, and she has been able to be a blessing to them.

If we had a thousand such persons, by the help of God we should see signs and wonders. There is no class of people, however hopeless or degraded, but can be reached, only we must lay ourselves out to reach them. Many Christians are asleep; we want to arouse them, so that they shall take a personal interest in those who are living in carelessness and sin. Let us lay aside all our prejudices. If God is working it matters little whether or not the work is done in the exact way that we would like to see it done, or in the way we have seen it done in the past.

Let there be one united cry going up to God, that He will revive His work in our midst. Let the work of revival begin with us who are Christians. Let us remove all the hindrances that come from ourselves. Then, by the help of the Spirit, we shall be able to reach these non-church goers, and multitudes will be brought into the kingdom of God.

CHAPTER II

LOVE, THE MOTIVE POWER FOR SERVICE

Let me call your attention to Paul's first letter to the Corinthians, thirteenth chapter: In reading this passage let us use the word "love" instead of "charity":—"Though I speak with the tongues of men and of angels, and have not love, I am become as sounding brass, or a tinkling cymbal. And though I have the gift of prophecy, and understand all mysteries, and all knowledge: and though I have all faith, so that I could remove mountains, and have not love, I am nothing. And though I bestow all my goods to feed the poor, and though I give my body to be burned, and have not love, it profiteth me nothing."

It is a great thing to be a prophet like Daniel, or Isaiah, or Elijah, or Elisha; but it is a greater thing, we are told here, to be full of love than to be filled with the spirit of prophecy. Mary of Bethany, who was so full of love, held a higher position than these great prophets did.

"Love suffereth long, and is kind; love envieth not; love vaunteth not itself, is not puffed up; Doth not behave itself unseemly, seeketh not her own, is not easily provoked, thinketh no evil; rejoiceth not in iniquity, but rejoiceth in the truth; beareth all things, believeth all things, hopeth all things, endureth all things. Love never faileth; but whether there be prophecies, they shall fail; whether there be tongues, they shall cease: whether there be knowledge, it shall vanish away. And now abideth faith, hope, love, these three; but the greatest of these is love."

The enemy had got into that little Church at Corinth established by Paul, and there was strife among the disciples. One said, "I am of Apollos;" another, "I am of Cephas;" and another, "I am of Paul." Paul saw that this sectarian strife and want of love among God's dear people would be disastrous to the Church of God, and so he wrote this letter. I have often said that if every true believer could move into this chapter and live in the spirit of it for twelve months, the Church of God would double its numbers within that time. One of the great obstacles in the way of God's work to-day is this want of love among those who are the disciples of the Lord Jesus Christ.

If we love a person we will not be pointing out his failings all the time. It is said: "Many rules of eloquence have been set forth, but, strange, to say, the first and most essential of all has been overlooked, namely, love. To address men well they must be loved much. Whatever they may be, be they ever so guilty, or indifferent, or ungrateful, or however deeply sunk in crime, before all, and above all, they must be loved. Love is the sap of the Gospel, the secret of lively and effectual preaching, the magic power of eloquence. The end of preaching is to reclaim the hearts of men to God, and nothing but love can find out the mysterious avenues which lead to the heart. If then you do not feel a fervent love and profound pity for humanity, be assured that the gift of Christian eloquence has been denied you. You will not win souls, neither will you acquire that most excellent of earthly sovereignties— sovereignty over human hearts. An Arab proverb runs thus—'The neck is bent by the sword, but heart is only bent by heart.' Love is irresistible."

Look at these words: "Love suffereth long, and is kind; love envieth not." How often it happens that if one outshines another there is apt to be envy in our hearts toward that one; we want a great deal of grace to keep it down. "Love vaunteth not itself, is not puffed up." One of the worst enemies that Christians have to contend with is this spirit of rivalry—this feeling, "Who shall be the greatest?"

Some years ago I read a book that did me a great deal of good. It was entitled, "The Training of the Twelve." The writer said that Christ spent most of His time during the three years He was engaged publicly about His Father's business in training twelve men. The training He gave them was very different from the training of the schools at the present day. The world teaches men that they must seek to be great; Christ taught that His disciples must be little; that in honor they must prefer one another; that they are not to be puffed up, not to harbor feelings of envy, but to be full of meekness and gentleness, and lowliness of heart.

When an eminent painter was requested to paint Alexander the Great so as to give a perfect likeness of the Macedonian conqueror, he felt a difficulty. Alexander, in his wars, had been struck by a sword, and across his forehead was an immense scar. The painter said: "If I retain the scar, it will be an offense to the admirers of the monarch, and if I omit it it will fail to be a perfect likeness. What shall I do?" He hit upon a happy expedient; he represented the Emperor leaning on his elbow, with his forefinger upon his brow, accidentally, as it seemed, covering the scar upon his forehead. Might not we represent each other with the finger of charity upon the scar, instead of representing the scar deeper and blacker than it really is? Christians may learn even from heathendom a lesson of charity, of human kindness and of love.

This spirit of seeking to be the greatest has nearly ruined the Church of God at different times in its history. If the Church had not been Divine it would have gone to pieces long ago. There is hardly any movement of reform to-day that has not been in danger of being thwarted and destroyed through this miserable spirit of ambition and self-seeking. May God enable us to get above this, to cast away our conceit and pride, and take Christ as our teacher, that He may show us in what spirit His work ought to be done.

One of the saddest things in the life of Christ was the working of this spirit among His disciples even in the last hours of His intercourse with them, and just before He was led away to be crucified. We read in the gospel by Luke: "But, behold, the hand of him that betrayeth Me is with Me on the table. And truly the Son of man goeth, as it was determined: but woe unto that man by whom He is betrayed! And they began to inquire among themselves, which of them it was that should do this thing. And there was also a strife among them which of them should be accounted the greatest. And He said unto them, "The kings of the Gentiles exercise lordship over them; and they that exercise authority upon them are called benefactors. But ye shall not be so: but he that is greatest among you, let him be as the younger; and he that is chief, as he that doth serve. For whether is greater, he that sitteth at meat, or he that serveth? Is not he that sitteth at meat? But I am among you as He that serveth."

Right there, on that memorable night when He had instituted the Last Supper, after they had been eating of the Passover Lamb, and the Saviour was on His way to the Cross,—even there this spirit arose among them: Who should be the greatest!

There is a charming tradition connected with the site on which the temple of Solomon was erected. It is said to have been occupied in common by two brothers, one of whom had a family—the other had none. On this spot was sown a field of wheat. On the evening succeeding the harvest—the wheat having been gathered in separate shocks—the elder brother said to his wife: "My younger brother is unable to bear the burden and heat of the day, I will arise, take of my shocks, and place with his without his knowledge." The younger brother being actuated by the same benevolent motives, said within himself: "My elder brother has a family, and I have none. I will arise, take of my shocks, and place it with his."

Judge of their mutual astonishment, when, on the following day, they found their respective shocks undiminished. This course of events transpired for several nights, when each resolved in his own mind to stand guard and solve the mystery. They did so; when, on the following night, they met each other half way between their respective shocks with their arms full. Upon ground hallowed by such associations as this was the temple of Solomon erected—so spacious and magnificent—the wonder and admiration of the world! Alas! in these days, how many would sooner steal their brother's whole shock than add to it a single sheaf!

If we want to be wise in winning souls and to be vessels meet for the Master's use we must get rid of the accursed spirit of self-seeking. That is the meaning of this chapter in Paul's letter. He told these Corinthians that a man might be full of faith and zeal; he might be very benevolent; but if he had not love he was like sounding brass and a tinkling cymbal. I believe many men might as well go into the pulpit and blow a tin horn Sabbath after Sabbath as go on preaching without love. A man may preach the truth; he may be perfectly sound in doctrine; but if there is no love in his heart going out to those whom he addresses, and if he is doing it professionally, the Apostle says he is only a sounding brass.

It is not always more work that we want so much as a better motive. Many of us do a good deal of work, but we must remember that God looks at the motive. The only tree on this earth that can produce fruit which is pleasing to God is the tree of love.

Paul in writing to Titus says: "Speak thou the things which become sound doctrine: that the aged men be sober, grave, temperate, sound in faith, in charity, (or love) in patience." What is the worth of a sermon, however sound in doctrine it may be, if it be not sound in love and in patience? What are our prayers worth without the spirit of love? People say: "Why is it that there is no blessing? Our minister's sermons and prayers are very good." Most likely you will find it is because the whole thing is done professionally. The words glisten like icicles in the sun, and they are as cold. There is not a spark of love in them. If that is the case there will be very little power. You may have your prayer-meetings, your praise meetings, your faith and hope meetings; you may talk about all these things;

but if there is no love mingled with them, God says you are as sounding brass and a tinkling cymbal.

Now a man may be a very good doctor and yet have no love for his patients. He may be a very clever and successful lawyer and yet have no love for his clients. A merchant may prosper greatly in business without caring at all about his customers. A man may be able to explain the wonderful mysteries of science or theology without any love. But no man can be a true worker for God, and a successful winner of souls without love. He may be a great preacher in the eyes of the world and have crowds flocking to hear him, but if love to God and to souls is not the motive power, the effects will all pass away like the morning cloud and the early dew.

It is said when the men of Athens went to hear Demosthenes they were always moved, and felt that they must go and fight Philip of Macedon. There was another orator of that day who could carry them away by his eloquence at the time, but when the oration was over, all the influence had gone; it was nothing but fine words. So a man may be very eloquent and have a great flow of language; he may sway the multitudes while they are under his influence; but if there is no love at the back of what he says, it will all go for nothing. It was Demosthenes' love for his country that stirred him, and then he stirred the people.

When we get on to the higher plane of love it will not be hard for us to work for the Lord. We will be glad to do anything, however small. God hates the great things in which love is not the motive power; but He delights in the little things that are prompted by a feeling of love. A cup of cold water given to a disciple in the spirit of love, is of far more value in God's sight than the taking of a kingdom, done out of ambition and vain glory.

I am getting sick and tired of hearing the word, duty, duty. You hear so many talk about it being their duty to do this and do that. My experience is that such Christians have very little success. Is there not a much higher platform than that of mere duty? Can we not engage in the service of Christ because we love Him? When that is the constraining power it is so easy to work. It is not hard for a mother to watch over a sick child. She does not look upon it as any hardship. You never hear Paul talking about what a hard time he had in his Master's service. He was constrained by love to Christ, and by the love of Christ to him. He counted it a joy to labor, and even to suffer, for his blessed Master.

Perhaps you say I ought not to talk against duty; because a good deal of work would not be done at all if it were not done from a sense of duty. But I want you to see what a poor, low motive that is, and how you may reach a higher plane of service.

I am thinking of going back to my home soon. I have in my mind an old, white-haired mother living on the banks of the Connecticut river, in the same little town where she has been for the last eighty years. Suppose when I return I take her some present, and when I give it to her I say: "You have been so very kind to me in the past that I thought it was my duty to bring you a present." What would she think? But how different it would be when I give it to her because of my strong love to her. How much more she would value it. So God wants His children to serve Him for something else than mere duty. He does not want us to feel that it is a hard thing to do His will.

Take an army that fights because it is compelled to do so; they will not gain many victories. But how different when they are full of love for their country and for their commanders. Then nothing can stand before them. Do not think you can do any work for Christ and hope to succeed if you are not impelled by love.

Napoleon tried to establish a kingdom by the force of arms. So did Alexander the Great, and Cæsar, and other great warriors; but they utterly failed. Jesus founded His kingdom on love, and it is going to stand. When we get on to this plane of love, then all selfish and unworthy motives will disappear, and our work will stand the fire when God shall put it to the test.

Another thing I want you to bear in mind. Love never looks to see what it is going to get in return. In the Gospel by Matthew we read of the parable of the man who went out to hire laborers that he might send them to work in his vineyard. After he had hired and sent out some in the morning, we are told that he found others standing idle later in the day, and he sent them also. It so happened that those who went out last got back first. Those that went out early in the morning supposed they would get more wages than those that went at the eleventh hour, and when they found they were only to get the same, they began to murmur and complain. But what was the good man's answer: "Friend, I do thee no wrong; didst not thou agree with me for a penny? Take that thine is, and go thy way; I will give unto this last, even as unto thee. Is it not lawful for me to do what I will with mine own? Is thine eye evil, because I am good? So the last shall be first, and the first last." I have generally found that those workers who are all the time looking to see how much they are going to get from the Lord are never satisfied. But love does its work and makes no bargain. Let us make no bargains with the Lord, but be ready to go out and do whatever He appoints.

I am sure if we go out cherishing love in our hearts for those we are going to try and reach, every barrier will be swept out of the way. Love begets love, just as hatred begets hatred. Love is the key to the human heart. Some one has said: "Light is for the mind, and love is for the heart." When you can reach men's hearts then you can turn them toward Christ. But we must first win them to ourselves.

You may have heard of the boy whose home was near a wood. One day he was in the wood, and he thought he heard the voice of another boy not far off. He shouted, "Hallo, there!" and the voice shouted back, "Hallo, there!" He did not know that it was the echo of his own voice, and he shouted again: "You are a mean boy!" Again the cry came back, "You are a mean boy!" After some more of the same kind of thing he went into the house and told his mother that there was a bad boy in the wood. His mother, who understood how it was, said to him: "Oh, no! You speak kindly to him, and see if he does not speak kindly to you." He went to the wood again and shouted: "Hallo, there!" "Hallo, there!" "You are a good boy." Of course the reply came, "You are a good boy." "I love you." "I love you," said the other voice.

You smile at that, but this little story explains the secret of the whole thing. Some of you perhaps think you have bad and disagreable neighbors; most likely the trouble is with yourself. If you love your neighbors they will love you. As I said before, love is the key that will unlock every human heart. There is no man or woman in all this land so low and so degraded but you can reach them with love, gentleness and kindness. It may take years to do it, but it can be done.

Love must be active. As some one has said: "A man may hoard up his money; he may bury his talents in a napkin; but there is one thing he cannot hoard up, and that is love." You cannot bury it. It must flow out. It cannot feed upon itself; it must have an object.

I remember reading a few years ago of something that happened when we had the yellow fever in one of the Southern cities. There was a family there who lived in a strange neighborhood where they had just moved. The father was stricken down with the fever. There were so many fatal cases happening that the authorities of the city did not stop to give them a decent burial. The dead-cart used to go through the street where the poor lived, and the bodies were carried away for burial.

The neighbors of this family were afraid, and no one would visit the house because of the fever. It was not long before the mother was stricken down. Before she died she called her boy to her, and said: "I will soon be gone, but when I am dead Jesus will come and take care of you." She had no one on earth to whom she could commit him. In a little while she, too, was gone, and they carried her body away to the cemetery. The little fellow followed her to the grave. He saw where they laid her, and then he came back to the house.

But he found it very lonely, and when it grew dark he got afraid and could not stay in the house. He went out and sat down on the step and began to weep. Finally he went back to the cemetery, and finding the lot where his mother was buried, he laid down and wept himself to sleep.

Next morning a stranger passing that way found him on the grave, still weeping. "What are you doing here, my boy?" "Waiting for the Savior." The man wanted to know what he meant, and the boy told the story of what his mother had said to him. It touched the heart of the stranger, and he said, "Well, my boy, Jesus has sent me to take care of you." The boy looked up and replied: "You have been a long while coming."

If we had the love of our Master do you tell me that these outlying masses would not be reached? There is not a drunkard who would not be reached. There is not a poor fallen one, or a blasphemer, or an atheist, but would be influenced for good. The atheists cannot get over the power of love. It will upset atheism and every false system quicker than anything else. Nothing will break the stubborn heart so quickly as the love of Christ.

I was in a certain home a few years ago; one of the household was a boy who, I noticed, was treated like one of the family, and yet he did not bear their name. One night I asked the lady of the house to explain to me what it meant. "I have noticed," I said, "that you treat him exactly like your own children, yet he is not your boy." "Oh no," she said, "he is not. It is quite true I treat him as my own child."

She went on to tell me his story. His father and mother were American missionaries in India; they had five children. The time came when the children had to be sent away from India, as they could not be educated there. They were to be sent to America for that purpose. The father and mother had been very much blessed in India, but they felt as though they could not give up their children. They thought they would leave their work in the foreign field and go back to America.

They were not blessed to the same extent in working at home as they had been in India. The natives were writing to them to return, and by and by they decided that the call was so loud the father must go back. The mother said to him: "I cannot let you go alone; I must go with you." "But how can you leave the children? You have never been separated from them." She said: "I can do it for Christ's sake." Thank God for such love as that.

When it was known they wanted to leave their children in good homes, this lady with whom I was staying said to the mother if she left one of them with her she would treat the child as her own. The mother came and stayed a week in the house to see that everything was right. The last morning came. When the carriage drove up to the door the mother said: "I want to leave my boy without shedding a tear; I cannot bear to have him think that it costs me tears to do what God has for me to do." My friend saw that there was a great struggle going on. Her room was adjoining this lady's, who told me she heard the mother crying: "O God, give me strength for the hour; help me now." She came downstairs with a beautiful smile on her face. She took her boy to her bosom, kissed him, and left him without a tear. She left all her children, and went back to labor for Christ in India; and from the shores of India she went up, before very long, to be with her Master. That is what a weak woman can do when love to Christ is the motive power. Some time after that dear boy passed away to be with the mother.

I was preaching in a certain city a few years ago, and I found a young man very active in bringing in the boys from the street into the meetings. If there was a hard case in the city he was sure to get hold of it. You would find him in the Inquiry Room with a whole crowd round him. I got to be very deeply interested in the young man and much attached to him. I found out that he was another son of that grand and glorious missionary. I found that all the sons were in training to go as foreign missionaries, to take the place of the mother and father, who had gone to their reward. It made such an impression on me that I could not shake it off. These boys have all gone to tell out among the heathen the story of Christ and His love.

I am convinced of this: When these hard-hearted people who now reject the Savior are thoroughly awake to the fact that love is prompting our efforts on their behalf, the hardness will begin to soften, and their stubborn wills will begin to bend. This key of love will unlock their hearts. We can turn them, by God's help, from the darkness of this world to the light of the Gospel.

Christ gave his disciples a badge. Some of you wear a blue ribbon and others wear a red ribbon, but the badge that Christ gave to his disciples was Love. "By this shall all men know that ye are My disciples, if ye have love one toward another." Love not only for those who are Christians, but love for the fallen. The Good Samaritan had love for the poor man who had fallen among thieves. If we are filled with such love as that, the world will soon find out that we are the followers of the Lord Jesus Christ. It will do more to upset infidelity and rebellion against God than anything else.

Speaking about hard cases being reached, reminds me that while I was in a home in London a young lady in that home felt that she was not doing as much for Christ as she would like, and she decided she would take a class of boys. She has now some fifteen or twenty of these lads, from thirteen to sixteen years of age—a very difficult age to deal with. This Christian young lady made up her mind that she would first try and win for herself the affection of these boys, and then seek to lead them to the Savior. It is a beautiful sight to see how she has won their young hearts for herself, and I believe she will win them all to a pure and Godly life. If we are willing to take up our work among the young with that spirit, these boys will be saved; and instead of helping to fill our prisons and poorhouses, they will become useful members of the Church of God, and a blessing to society.

I have a friend who has a large Sabbath-school. He made up his mind when he began that if a boy did not have a good training in his own home, he could not get it anywhere else except in the Sabbath-school; and he resolved that, if possible, when a boy was refractory he would not turn him adrift.

He had a boy come to the school whom no teacher seemed able to manage. One after another would come to the Superintendent and say: "You must take him out of my class; he is demoralizing all the others; he uses profane language, and he is doing more harm than all the good I can do." At last my friend made up his mind he would read the boy's name out and have him expelled publicly.

He told a few of the teachers what he was going to do, but a wealthy young lady said: "I wish you would let me try the boy; I will do all I can to win him." My friend said to himself he was sure she would not have patience with him very long, but he put the boy in her class as she requested. The little fellow very soon broke the rules in the class, and she corrected him. He got so angry that he lost his temper and spat in her face. She quietly took a handkerchief and wiped her face. At the close of the lesson she asked him if he would walk home with her when school was over. No, he said, he didn't want to speak to her. He was not coming back to that old school any more. She asked if he would let her walk along with him. No, he wouldn't. Well, she said, she was sorry he was going, but if he would call at her house on Tuesday morning and ring the front door bell, there would be a little parcel waiting for him. She would not be at home herself, but if he asked the servant he would receive it. He replied: "You can keep your old parcel; I don't want it." However she thought he would be there.

By Tuesday morning the little fellow had got over his mad fit. He came to the house and rang the door bell; the servant handed him the parcel. When he opened it he found it contained a little vest, a necktie, and, best of all, a note written by the teacher. She told him how every night and every morning since he had been in her class she had been praying for him. Now that he was going to leave her she wanted him to remember that as long as she lived she would pray for him, and she hoped he would grow up to be a good man.

Next morning the little fellow was in the drawing-room waiting to see her before she came downstairs from her bedroom. She found him there crying as if his heart would break. She asked him kindly what was the trouble. "Oh," he said, "I have had no peace since I got your letter. You have been so kind to me and I have been so unkind to you; I wish you would forgive me." Said my friend, the Superintendent, "There are about eighteen hundred children in the school, and there is not a better boy among the whole of them."

Can we not do the same as that young lady did? Shall we not reconsecrate ourselves now to God and to his service?

> Had I the tongues of Greeks and Jews,
> And nobler speech than angels use:
> If love be absent, I am found
> Like tinkling brass, an empty sound.
>
> Were I inspired to preach and tell
> All that is done in heaven and hell—
> Or could my faith the world remove:
> Still I am nothing without love.
>
> Should I distribute all my store
> To feed the hungry, clothe the poor
> Or give my body to the flame,
> To gain a martyr's glorious name:
>
> If love to God and love to men
> Be absent, all my hopes are vain;
> Nor tongues, nor gifts, nor fiery zeal,
> The work of love can e'er fulfill.

Dr. Watts

CHAPTER III

FAITH AND COURAGE

The key note of all our work for God should be Faith. In all my life I have never seen men or women disappointed in receiving answers to their prayers, if those persons were full of faith, and had good grounds for their faith. Of course we must have a warrant in Scripture for what we expect. I am sure we have a good warrant in coming together to pray for a blessing on our friends and on our neighbors.

Unbelief is as much an enemy to the Christian as it is to the unconverted. It will keep back the blessing now as much as it did in the days of Christ. We read that in one place Christ could not do many mighty works because of their unbelief. If Christ could not do this, how can we expect to accomplish anything if the people of God are unbelieving? I contend that God's children are alone able to hinder God's work. Infidels, atheists, and sceptics cannot do it. Where there is union, strong faith, and expectation among Christians, a mighty work is always done.

In Hebrews we read that without faith it is impossible to please God. "For he that cometh to God must believe that He is, and that He is a Rewarder of them that diligently seek Him." That is addressed to us who are Christians as much as to those who are seeking God for the first time. We are all of us seeking a blessing on our friends. We want God to revive us, and also that the outlying masses may be reached. We read in this passage that God blesses those who "diligently seek Him." Let us diligently seek Him to-day; let us have great faith; and let our expectation be from God.

I remember when I was a boy, in the spring of the year, when the snow had melted away on the New England hills where I lived, I used to take a certain kind of glass and hold it up to the warm rays of the sun. These would strike on it, and I would set the woods on fire. Faith is the glass that brings the fire of God out of heaven. It was faith that drew the fire down on Carmel and burned up Elijah's offering. We have the same God to-day, and the same faith. Some people seem to think that faith is getting old, and that the Bible is wearing out. But the Lord will revive his work now; and we shall be able to set the world on fire if each believer has a strong and simple faith.

In the eleventh chapter of the Epistle to the Hebrews the writer brings up one worthy after another, and each of them was a man or a woman of faith; they made the world better by living in it. Listen to this description of what was accomplished by these men and women of faith: "Who through faith subdued kingdoms, wrought righteousness, obtained promises, stopped the mouths of lions, quenched the violence of fire, escaped the edge of the sword, out of weakness were made strong, waxed valiant in fight, turned to flight the armies of the aliens. Women received their dead raised to life again; and others were tortured, not accepting deliverance; that they might obtain a better resurrection: and others had trial of cruel mockings and scourgings, yea, moreover, of bonds and imprisonment. They were stoned, they were sawn asunder, were tempted, were slain with the sword: they wandered about in sheepskins and goatskins, being destitute, afflicted, tormented (of whom the world was not worthy): they wandered in deserts, and in mountains, and in dens and caves of the earth. And these all, having obtained a good report through faith, received not the promise: God having provided some better thing for us, that they without us should not be made perfect."

Surely no child of God can read these words without being stirred. It is said that "women received their dead raised to life again." Many of you have children who have gone far astray, and have been taken captive by strong drink, or led away by their lusts and passions; and you have become greatly discouraged about them. But if you have faith in God they may be raised up as from the dead, and brought back again. The wanderers may be reclaimed; the drunkards and the harlots may be reached and saved. There is no man or woman, however low he or she may have sunk, but can be reached.

We ought in these days to have far more faith than Abel, or Enoch, or Abraham had. They lived away on the other side of the Cross. We talk about the faith of Elijah, and the Patriarchs and Prophets; but they lived in the dim light of the past, while we are in the full blaze of Calvary, and the Resurrection. When we look back and think of what Christ did, how He poured out His blood that men might be saved, we ought to go forth in His strength and conquer the world. Our God is able to do great and mighty things.

You remember that the Roman Centurion sent for Christ to heal his servant; when the Savior drew near, the Centurion sent to Him to say that He need not take the trouble to come into his house; all that was needed was that He should speak the word and his servant would live. Probably he thought that if Christ had the power to create worlds, to say "Let there be light," and there was light, to make the sea and the earth bring forth abundantly, He could easily say the word and raise up his sick servant. We are told that when Christ received the Roman soldier's message He marvelled at his faith. Dear friends, let us have faith at this moment that God will do great things in our midst.

Caleb and Joshua were men of faith. They were worth more to Israel than all the camp of unbelievers and the other ten spies put together. We read that Moses sent out twelve men to spy out the land. Let me say that faith never sends out any spies. You may perhaps reply that Moses was commanded by God to send them out; but we read that it was because of the hardness of their hearts. If they had believed in God, they would have taken possession of the land at Kadesh Barnea. I suppose these twelve men were chosen because they were leading men and influential men in the twelve tribes.

After they had been gone some thirty days they came back with what we might call a minority and a majority report. All the twelve admitted that the land was a good land, but the ten said, "We are not able to take it. We saw giants there—the sons of Anak." You can see these ten spies in camp the night they returned; great crowds are gathered around them listening to their reports. Probably there were very few gathered to hear Caleb and Joshua. It really seems sometimes that people are much more ready to believe a lie than to believe the truth. So these unbelieving men gathered around the ten spies. One of them is describing the giants in the land, and he says: "Why, I had to look right up in order to see their faces; they made the earth tremble at their tread. The mountains and valleys are full of them. Then we saw great walled cities. We are not able to take the land."

But Caleb and Joshua had quite a different story to tell. Those mighty giants seemed to be as grasshoppers in their sight. These men of faith remembered how God had delivered them out of the hand of Pharaoh and brought them through the Red Sea; how He had given them bread from heaven to eat, and water to drink from the rock in the wilderness. If He marched with them surely they could go right up and take possession of the land. So they said: "Let us go up at once and possess it; we are well able to take it."

What do we see in the Church of God to-day? About ten out of every twelve professed Christians are looking at the giants, at the walls, and at the difficulties in the way. They say: "We are not able to accomplish this work. We might do it if there were not so many drinking saloons, and so much drunkenness, and so many atheists and opposers." Let us not give head to these unbelieving professors. If we have faith in God we are well able to go up and possess the land for Christ. God always delights to honor faith.

It may be some sainted weak woman, some bed-ridden one who is not able to attend the meetings, who will bring down the blessing. In the day when every man's work is tested, it may be seen that some hidden one who honored God by a simple faith was the one who caused such a blessing to descend upon our cities as shall shake the land from end to end.

Again, in these Bible histories we find that faith is always followed by courage. Caleb and Joshua were full of courage, because they were men of faith. Those who have been greatly used of God in all ages have been men of courage. If we are full of faith we shall not be full of fear, distrusting God all the while. That is the trouble with the Church of Christ to-day—there are so many who are fearful, because they do not believe that God is going to use them. What we need is to have the courage that will compel us to move forward. Perhaps if we do this we may have to go against the advice of lukewarm Christians. There are some who never seem to do anything but object, because the work is not always carried on exactly according to their ideas. They will say: "I do not think that is the best way to do things." They are very fruitful in raising objections to any plans that can be suggested. If any onward step is taken they are ready to throw cold water on it; they will suggest all kinds of difficulties. We want to have such faith and courage as shall enable us to move forward without waiting for these timid unbelievers.

In the second book of Chronicles we read that King Asa had to go right against his father and mother; it took a good deal of courage to do that. He removed his mother from being queen, and cut down the idols and burnt them. There are times when we have to go against those who ought to be our best friends. Is it not time for us to launch out into the deep? I have never seen people go out into the lanes and alleys, into the hedges and highways, and try to bring the people in, but the Lord gave His blessing. If a man has the courage to go right to his neighbor and speak to him about his soul, God is sure to smile upon the effort. The person who is spoken to may wake up cross, but that is not always a bad sign. He may write a letter next day and apologize. At any rate it is better to wake him up in this way than that he should continue to slumber on to death and ruin.

You notice when God was about to deliver Israel out of the hand of the Midianites, how he taught this lesson to Gideon. Gideon had gathered around him an army of thirty-two thousand men. He may probably have counted them, and when he knew that the Midianites had an army of a hundred and thirty-five thousand he said to himself: "My army is too small; I am afraid I shall not succeed." But the Lord's thoughts were different. He said to Gideon: "You have too many men." So He told him that all those among the thirty-two thousand who were fearful and afraid might go back to their own homes, to their wives and their mothers; let them step to the rear. No sooner had Gideon given this command than twenty-two thousand men wheeled out of line. It may be Gideon thought the Lord had made a mistake as he saw his army melt away. If two-thirds of a great audience were to rise and go out you would think they were all going.

The Lord said: "Gideon, you have too many men yet. Take your men down to the brook and try them once more. All those who take the water up in their hands and drink as they pass by can stay; those who stoop down to drink can go back." Again he gave the word, and nine thousand seven hundred wheeled out of line and went to the rear, so that Gideon was left with three hundred men. But this handful of men whose hearts beat true to the God of heaven, and who were ready to go forward in His name, were worth more than all the others who were all the time sowing seeds of discontent and predicting defeat. Nothing will discourage an army like that. Nothing is more discouraging in a Church than to have a number of the people all the time expecting disaster and saying: "We do not think this effort will amount to anything; it is not according to our ideas."

It would be a good thing for the Church of God if all the fearful and faithless ones were to step to the rear, and let those who are full of faith and courage take their empty pitchers and go forward against the enemy. This little band of three hundred men who were left with Gideon routed the Midianites; but it was not their own might that gave them the victory. It was "the sword of the Lord and of Gideon." If we go on in the Name of the Lord, and trusting to His might, we shall succeed.

Before Moses went up to heaven he did all he could to encourage Joshua, to strengthen and cheer him. There was no sign of jealousy in the heart of Moses, although he was not permitted to go into the land. He went up to the top of Pisgah and saw that it was a good land; and he tried to encourage Joshua to go forward and take possession of it. After Moses had gone, we read that three times in one chapter God said to Joshua: "Be of good courage." God cheered his servant; "There shall not any man be able to stand before thee all the days of thy life." Soon after that Joshua took a walk around the walls of Jericho. As he walked around he saw a man stand before him with a drawn sword in his hand. Joshua was not afraid, but he said: "Art thou for us or for our adversaries?" His courage was rewarded, for the man replied: "As Captain of the host of the Lord am I now come." He had been sent to encourage him and to lead him on to victory.

So you will find all through the Scriptures that God uses those who have courage, and not those who are looking for defeat.

Another thought: I never knew a case where God used a discouraged man or woman to accomplish any great thing for Him. Let a minister go into the pulpit in a discouraged frame of mind and it becomes contagious. It will soon reach the pews, and the whole church will become discouraged. So with a Sabbath-school teacher; I never knew a worker of any kind who was full of discouragement and who met with success in the Lord's work. It seems as if God cannot make any use of such a man.

I remember a man telling me he preached for a number of years without any result. He used to say to his wife as they went to church that he knew the people would not believe anything he said; and there was no blessing. At last he saw his error; he asked God to help him, and took courage, and then the blessing came. "According to your faith it shall be unto you." This man had expected nothing and he got just what he expected. Dear friends, let us expect that God is going to use us. Let us have courage and go forward, looking to God to do great things.

Elijah on Mount Carmel was one man; Elijah under the juniper tree was quite another man. In the one case he was a giant, and nothing could stand before him. When he lost heart and got terrified at Jezebel's message, and wished himself dead, God could not use him. The Lord had to go to him and say: "What doest thou here, Elijah?" I wish God would speak to many professing Christians who have their harps on the willows, and are out of communion with Him, so that they are of no use in His cause.

When Peter denied his Master he was a very different man from what he was on the day of Pentecost. He got out of communion with his Lord, and the word of a servant nearly frightened him out of his life. He denied his Master with oaths and cursing. How terribly a man falls when he loses faith and courage.

But he was restored; look at him on the day of Pentecost. If that maid whose question made him tremble had been present, and heard him preach the marvellous sermon recorded in the Acts, I can imagine she would be the most amazed person in all Jerusalem, "Why," she says, "I saw him a few days ago, and he was terribly alarmed at being called a disciple of Christ; now he stands up boldly for this same Christ; he has no shame now." God used him mightily on the day of Pentecost, as he preached to that vast congregation, some of whom were the very murderers of his Lord and Master. But he could not use Peter till he had repented of his cowardice and had been restored to faith and courage. So when any man who is working for Christ loses heart and gets discouraged, the Lord has to lay him aside.

I remember a number of years ago I got cast down for a good many weeks. One Sunday in particular I had preached and there did not seem to be any result. On the Monday I was very much cast down. I was sitting in my study and was looking at myself, brooding over my want of success. A young man called upon me, who had a Bible class of 100 adults in the Sabbath-school which I conducted. As he came in I could see he was away upon the mountain top, while I was down in the valley. Said he to me, "What kind of a day did you have yesterday?" "Very poor; I had no success, and I feel quite cast down. How did you get on?" "Oh, grandly; I never had a better day." "What was your subject?" "I had the life and character of Noah. Did you ever preach on Noah? Did you ever study up his life?" "Well, no; I do not know as ever I made it a special study." I thought I knew pretty well all there was about him in the Bible; you know all that is told us about him is contained in a few verses. "If you never studied it before, you had better do it now. It will do you good. Noah was a wonderful character."

When the young man went out I got my Bible and some other books, and read all I could find about Noah, I had not been reading long before the thought came stealing over me: Here was a man who toiled on for a hundred and twenty years and never had a single convert outside of his own family. Yet he did not get discouraged. I closed up my Bible; the cloud had gone; I started out and went to the noon prayer-meeting. I had not been there long when a man got up and said he had come from a little town in Illinois. On the day before he had admitted a hundred young converts to Church membership. As he was speaking I said to myself: "I wonder what Noah would have given if he could have heard that. He never had any such result as that to his labors."

Then in a little while a man who sat right behind me stood up. His hand was on the seat, and I felt it shake; I could realise that the man was trembling. He said: "I wish you would pray for me; I would like to become a Christian." Thought I to myself: "wonder what Noah would have given if he had heard that. He never heard a single soul asking God for mercy, yet he did not get discouraged." I have never hung my harp on the willows since that day. Let us ask God to take away the clouds of fear and unbelief; let us get out of Doubting Castle; let us move forward courageously in the name of our God and expect to see results.

If you cannot engage in any active work yourselves you can do a good deal by cheering on others. Some people not only do nothing, but they are all the time throwing discouragement on others, in every forward step they take. If you meet with them they seem to chill you through and through. I think I would as soon face the east wind in Edinburgh in the month of March, as come in contact with some of these so-called Christians. Perhaps they are speaking about some effort that has been made, and they say: "Well, yes, a good deal of work was done, but then many were not reached at all." Such and such a thing ought to have been done in a different way, and I know not what. They are all the time looking at the dark side.

Let us not give heed to these gloomy and discouraging remarks. In the name of our great Commander let us march on to battle and to victory. There are some generals whose name alone is worth more than a whole army of ten thousand men. In our army in the Civil War there were some whose presence sent a cheer all along the line. As they passed on cheer upon cheer went up. The men knew who was going to lead them, and they were sure of having success. "The boys" liked to fight under such generals as that. Let us encourage ourselves in the Lord, and encourage each other; then we shall have good success.

We read in the book of First Chronicles that Joab cheered on those who were helping him in warfare. "Be of good courage, and let us behave ourselves valiantly for our people and for the cities of our God; and let the Lord do that which is good in His sight." Let us go forward in this spirit, and the Lord will make us to triumph over our foes. If we cannot be in the battle ourselves let us not seek to discourage others. A Highland chief of the M'Gregor clan fell wounded at the battle of Sheriff-Muir. Seeing their leader fall, the clan wavered, and gave the foe an advantage. The old chieftain, perceiving this, raised himself on his elbow, while the blood streamed from his wounds, and cried out, "I am not dead, my children; I am looking at you to see you do your duty." This roused them to new energy and almost superhuman effort. So, when our strength fails and our hearts sink within us, the Captain of our salvation cries: "Lo, I am with you alway, even to the end of the world. I will never leave nor forsake thee. Be thou faithful unto death, and I will give thee a crown of life."

A friend of mine was telling me that a worker came to him very much cast down. Everything was going wrong, and he was greatly depressed. My friend turned upon him and said: "Do you have any doubt about the final result of things? Is Jesus Christ going to set up His Kingdom, and reign from the rivers to the ends of the earth? Is He going to succeed or not?" The man said that of course Christ was going to triumph; he had never thought of it in that light. If people would sometimes take a look into the future and remember the promises, they would not be cast down. Dear friends, Christ is going to reign. Let us go out and do the work He has given us to do. If it happens to be dark round about us, let us remember it is light somewhere else. If we are not succeeding just as we would like, others, it may be, are succeeding better.

Think of the opportunities we have, compared with the early Christians. Look at the mighty obstacles they had to encounter—how they had often to seal their testimony with their blood. See what Peter had to fight against on the day of Pentecost, when the people looked on him with scorn. The disciples in those days had no committee to put up large buildings for their use, in which they could preach. They had no band of ministers sitting near by, to pray for them, and help them and cheer them on. Yet look at the wonderful results of Peter's preaching on the day of Pentecost.

Look at the dense darkness that surrounded Martin Luther in Germany. Look at the difficulties that John Knox had to meet with in Scotland. Yet these men did a mighty and a lasting work for God in their day and generation; we are reaping the blessed fruits of their faithful labors even now. Look at the darkness that brooded over England in the days of Wesley and Whitefield. See how God blessed their efforts; and yet they had a great many obstacles to contend with that we do not have in these days. They went forward with strong and courageous hearts, and the Lord gave them success.

I believe if our forefathers who lived in the last century could come back to this world in the flesh, they would be amazed to see the wonderful opportunities that we have. We have a great many advantages they did not possess, and probably did not dream of. We live in a grand and glorious day. It took John Wesley months to cross the Atlantic; now we can do it a few days. Think of the power of the printing press in these days; we can print and scatter sermons to all the corners of the earth. Look at the marvellous facilities that we have in the electric telegraph, Then we can take the railway train and go and preach at a distance of hundreds of miles in a few hours. Am I not right in saying that we live in a glorious day? Let us not be discouraged, but let us use all these wonderful opportunities, and honor God by expecting great things. If we do we will not be disappointed. God is ready and willing to work, if we are ready and willing to let Him, and to be used by Him.

It may be that some are old and feeble, and are saying to themselves: "I wish I were young again; I would like to go out into the thick of the battle." But any one, young or old, can go into the homes of the people and invite them to come out to the meetings. There are large halls everywhere with plenty of room; there are many who will help sing the Gospel. The Gospel will also be preached, and there are many people who might be induced to come, who will not go out to the regular places of worship.

If you are not able to go and invite the people, as I have said, you can give a word of cheer to others, and wish them Godspeed. Many a time when I have come down from the pulpit, some old man, trembling on the very verge of another world, living perhaps on borrowed time, has caught hold of my hand, and in a quavering voice said, "God bless you!" How the words have cheered and helped me. Many of you can speak a word of encouragement to the younger friends, if you are too feeble to work yourselves.

Then again, you can pray that God will bless the words that are spoken and the efforts that are made. It is very easy to preach when others are all the time praying for you and sympathizing with you, instead of criticising and finding fault.

You have heard the story, I suppose, of the child who was rescued from the fire that was raging in a house away up in the fourth story. The child came to the window, and as the flames were shooting up higher and higher it cried out for help. A fireman started up the ladder of the fire-escape to rescue the child from its dangerous position. The wind swept the flames near him, and it was getting so hot that he wavered, and it looked as if he would have to return without the child. Thousands looked on, and their hearts quaked at the thought of the child having to perish in the fire, as it must do if the fireman did not reach it. Some one in the crowd cried, "Give him a cheer!" Cheer after cheer went up, and as the man heard them he gathered fresh courage. Up he went into the midst of the smoke and the fire, and brought down the child in safety. If you cannot go and rescue the perishing yourselves, you can at least pray for those who do, and cheer them on. If you do, the Lord will bless the effort.

"They helped every one his neighbor; and every one said to his brother, 'Be of good courage.'"

> We are living, we are dwelling
> In a grand and awful time,

In an age on ages telling—
To be living is sublime.

Oh, let all the soul within you
For the truth's sake go abroad!
Strike! let every nerve and sinew
Tell on ages—tell for God!

> Coxe

CHAPTER IV

FAITH REWARDED

"And it came to pass on a certain day, as He was teaching, that there were Pharisees and doctors of the law sitting by, which were come out of every town of Galilee, and Judea and Jerusalem; and the power of the Lord was present to heal them. And, behold, men brought in a bed a man which was taken with a palsy; and they sought means to bring him in, and to lay him before Him. And when they could not find by what way they might bring him in, because of the multitude, they went upon the house-top, and let him down through the tiling with his couch into the midst before Jesus. And when He saw their faith, He said unto him, 'Man, thy sins are forgiven thee.'"

All the three evangelists, Matthew, Mark and Luke, record this miracle. I have noticed that when any two or three of the Gospel writers record a miracle it is to bring out some important truth. It seems to me that the truth the Lord would teach us here is this: The honor He put upon the faith of these four men who brought the palsied man to him for healing. Whether the palsied man himself had any faith we are not told; it was when He saw "their faith" that His power was put forth to cure the sick of the palsy.

I want to say to all Christian workers, that if the Lord sees our faith for those whom we wish to be blessed, He will honor it. He has never disappointed the faith of any of His children yet. You cannot find an instance in the Bible, where any man or woman has exercised true faith in God, where it has not been honored. Nothing that the Savior found when He was on this sin-cursed earth pleased Him so much as to see the faith of His disciples; nothing refreshed His heart so much.

We read in the Gospel narrative that there was a great stir in the town of Capernaum at this time. A few weeks before, the Savior had been cast out of his native town of Nazareth. He had come down to Capernaum, and the whole country was greatly moved. His star was just rising, and His fame was being spread abroad. Peter's wife's mother had been healed by a word. The servant of an officer in the Roman army had been raised up from a sick bed, and the Savior had performed many other wonderful miracles. Men had come to Capernaum from every town in Galilee, and Judæa, and from Jerusalem. They had gathered together to look into these wonderful events that were occurring. The voice of John the Baptist had been ringing through the land, proclaiming to the people that a Prophet would soon make His appearance, whose shoe latchet he was not worthy to unloose. While the Baptist was telling out this message the Prophet Himself made His appearance in the northern part of the country, and all these wonderful things were transpiring.

The Pharisees and doctors of the law had come to Capernaum to look into the reports that were spread abroad. The house where they were gathered was filled to overflowing, and these wise men were listening to the Savior's teaching. Many of them hardly believed a word that He said. It may be there were some believing ones among these wise men. Nicodemus and Joseph of Arimathea may have been there: if so, they were not yet known as disciples of Jesus.

The writer of the Gospel says: "The power of the Lord was present to heal them." We are not told, however, that one of them was healed. So it is very often now. The power of the Lord may be present to heal in these gatherings; yet many will come and go, wondering what it all means, and without being healed of their spiritual diseases. What we need is to have the power of God in our midst.

A man came into one of our meetings in London. He got into a part of the hall where he could not hear a word of what was spoken or sung; he could not even hear the text or the portion of Scripture that was read. There he had to sit through the service, so to speak, shut up alone with himself. A little while after he told some one that as he sat there God had revealed Himself to him, and spoken peace to his soul. There is such a thing as the power of God being present to heal, though men may not hear the voice of their fellowman.

These four men were real workers. They were worth more than a houseful of these Pharisees and doctors of the law who came merely to criticise and look on. I do not know who the four men were, but I have always had a great admiration for them. It may be one of them had been blind and the Lord had given him his sight. The other may have been lame from his birth; when the Master restored him to strength, he thought he would like to use it in bringing some one else to be healed. The third man may have been a cured leper, and he wished to help in getting some other afflicted one cured. Perhaps this palsied man was his next-door neighbor. The fourth man, it may be, had been deaf and dumb, and he thought he would employ his hearing and his speech in helping some one else. These four young converts said to themselves: "Let us bring our sick neighbor to Christ." The palsied man may have said he had no faith in Christ. But these four friends told him how they had been cured, and if the Master could heal them surely He could heal a palsied man.

Now it seems to me nothing will wake up a man quicker than to have four persons after him in one day. People are sometimes afraid that they will entrench on each other's ground if more than one worker happens to call at the same house. For my part, I wish that every family had about forty invitations to each meeting.

I lately heard of a man, a non-churchgoer, who did not believe in the Bible or religious things. Some one who was distributing tickets asked him if he would go to the meetings. He got quite angry. No, he would not go; he did not believe in the thing at all; he would not be seen in such a crowd. A second man came along, not knowing that any one had been before him, and asked if he would accept a ticket for the meetings. The man was still angry, and, as we would sometimes say, he "gave him a piece of his mind." He told him to keep his tickets. By-and-by a third man called and said: "Would you take a ticket for these meetings?" The man by this time had got thoroughly waked up, but yet he declined to receive the ticket. He went into a shop to buy something. The man in the shop put a ticket for the meetings into the packet; when the customer got home and opened it, lo and behold there was a ticket! He got so roused up that he went, not to our meeting, but to a neighboring church. I do not know that he has come clean out, but I believe he is, at any rate, in a hopeful condition.

If one visit does not wake up a man whom you want to reach, send a second visitor after him; if that has no effect, send a third, and a fourth, and a fifth, and a sixth, and a seventh; go on in that way day after day. It is a great thing to save one man, to get him out of the pit, to have his feet set fast on a rock, and a new song put in his mouth. Nothing will rouse an indifferent man quicker than to have a number of friends after him. If you cannot bring him yourself, get others to help you.

These four men found an obstacle in the way. The door of the house was blocked, and they could not get near the Master. They may have asked some of these philosophers to stand aside; but no, they would not do that. They would not disturb themselves about a sick man. Many people will not go into the kingdom of God themselves, and they will throw obstacles in the way of others. After trying probably for some time to get in, these four men began to devise another plan. If it had been some of us, most likely we would have got quite discouraged, and carried the man back to his home.

These men had faith, and perseverance too. They are going to get their friend to Christ some way. If they cannot get him through the door, they will find a way through the roof! "Zeal without knowledge," people say. I would a good deal rather have that than knowledge without zeal. You can see them pulling and tugging away at the burden. If you have ever tried to carry a wounded man up a flight of stairs you will know it is not an easy matter. But these four men were not to be defeated, and at last he is up there on the roof.

Now, the question was, "How can we get him down?" They began to tear up the tiling. I can see those wise men looking up and saying to one another: "This is a strange performance; we have never seen anything like this in the temple or in any synagogue we were ever in. It is altogether out of the regular order. These men must be carried away with fanaticism. Why, they have made a hole large enough to let a man through. Suppose a sudden shower were to come, it would spoil the house."

But these four workers were terribly in earnest. They let the bier, on which the man was lying, down into the room. They laid their friend right at the feet of Jesus Christ; a good place to lay him, was it not? Perhaps some of you have a sceptical son or an unbelieving husband, or some other member of your family, that scoffs at the Bible and sneers at Christianity. Lay them at the feet of Jesus, and He will honor your faith.

"When He saw their faith." I suppose these men were looking down to see what was about to take place Christ looked at them, and when He saw their faith He said to the palsied man: "Son, be of good cheer; thy sins are forgiven thee." That was more than they expected; they only thought of his body being made whole. So let us bring our friends to Christ, and we shall get more than we expect. The Lord met this man's deepest need first. It may be his sins had brought on the palsy, so the Lord forgave the man's sin first of all.

The wise men began to reason within themselves: "Who is this that forgiveth sins?" The Master could read their thoughts as easily as we can read a book. "Is it easier to say, 'Thy sins be forgiven thee,' or 'Rise up and walk?' But that ye may know that the Son of Man hath power on earth to forgive sins, He said unto the sick of the palsy, 'I say unto thee, arise; take up thy bed and go into thine house.'" The man leaped to his feet, made whole. He rolled up the old bed, swung it across his shoulders, and went to his house. Depend upon it, these philosophers who would not make way in order to let him in stood aside pretty quick to let him go out. No need for him to go out by way of the roof; he went out by the door.

Dear friends, let us have faith for those we bring to Christ. Let us believe for them if they will not believe for themselves. It may be there are those here who do not believe in the Bible, or in the Gospel of the Son of God. Let us bring them to Christ in the arms of our faith. He is unchangeable—"the same yesterday, today, and for ever." Let us look for great things. Let us expect the dead to be raised, the harlots reclaimed, the drunkards saved, and the devils cast out. I believe men are possessed of evil spirits now, just as much as when the Son of God was on earth. We want to bring them right to the Lord Jesus Christ, that He may heal and save them. Let this cursed unbelief be swept out of the way, and let us come to God as one man, looking for and expecting signs and wonders to be done in the name of Jesus. He can perform miracles to-day, and He will if we ask Him to fulfill His promises. "He is able to save to the uttermost."

And let me say to any unsaved man that God has the power to save you from your sins to-day. If you want to be converted, come right to the Master as did the leper of old. He said, "Lord, if Thou wilt Thou canst make me clean." Christ honored his faith, and said, "I will; be thou clean." Notice—the man put "if" in the right place. "If Thou will." He did not doubt the power of the Son of God. The father who brought his son to Christ said, "If Thou canst, have compassion upon him." The Lord straightened out his theology then and there; "If thou canst believe." Mother, can you believe for your boy? If you can, the Lord will speak the word, and it shall be done.

It will be a good thing for us to get right down at the feet of the Master, like the poor woman who went to Elisha and told him of her dead child. He asked his servant to take his staff and lay it upon the dead child. But the mother would not leave the prophet. He wanted her to go with the servant, but she would not be satisfied with the prophet's staff, or even with his servant; she wanted the master himself. So Elisha went with her; it was a good thing he did, for the servant could not raise the child.

We want to get beyond the staff and beyond the servant, right to the heart of the Master Himself. Let us bring our palsied friends to Him. It is said of Christ that in one place He could not do many mighty works there because of their unbelief. Let us ask Him to take away from us this cursed unbelief, that hinders the blessing from coming down, and prevents those who are sick of the palsy of sin from being saved.

> "The faith that works by love,
> And purifies the heart,
> A foretaste of the joys above
> To mortals can impart;
> It bears us through this earthly strife,
> And triumphs in immortal life."

CHAPTER V

ENTHUSIASM

"Awake thou that sleepest, and arise from the dead, and Christ shall give thee light." I want to apply these words to the children of God. If the lost are to be reached by the Gospel of the Son of God, Christianity must be more aggressive than it has been in the past. We have been on the defensive long enough; the time has come for us to enter on a war of aggression. When we as children of God wake up and go to work in the vineyard, then those who are living in wickedness all about us will be reached; but not in any other way. You may go to mass meetings and discuss the question of "How to reach the masses," but when you have done with discussion you have to go back to personal effort. Every man and woman who loves the Lord Jesus Christ must wake up to the fact that he or she has a mission in the world, in this work of reaching the lost.

A man may talk in his sleep, and it seems to me that there is a good deal of that kind of thing now in the Lord's work. A man may even preach in his sleep. A friend of mine sat up in his bed one night and preached a sermon right through. He was sound asleep all the time. Next morning his wife told him all about it. He preached the same sermon in his church the next Sabbath morning; I have it in print, and a good sermon it is. So a man may not only talk but actually preach in his sleep. There are many preachers in these days who are fast asleep.

There is one thing, however, that we must remember; a man cannot work in his sleep. There is no better way to wake up a Church than to set it to work. One man will wake up another in waking himself up. Of course the moment we begin a work of aggression, and declare war with the world, the flesh, and the devil, some wise head will begin to shake, and there will be the cry, "Zeal without knowledge!" I think I have heard that objection ever since I commenced the Christian life. I heard of some one who was speaking the other day of something that was to be done, and who said he hoped zeal would be tempered with moderation. Another friend very wisely replied that he hoped moderation would be tempered with zeal. If that were always the case, Christianity would be like a red hot ball rolling over the face of the earth. There is no power on earth that can stand before the onward march of God's people when they are in dead earnest.

In all ages God has used those who were in earnest. Satan always calls idle men into his service. God calls active and earnest—not indolent men. When we are thoroughly aroused and ready for His work, then He will take us up and use us. You remember where Elijah found Elisha; he was ploughing in the field—he was at work. Gideon was at the threshing floor. Moses was away in Horeb looking after the sheep. None of these eminent servants of God were indolent men; what they did, they did with all their might. We want such men and women nowadays. If we cannot do God's work with all the knowledge we would like, let us at any rate do it with all the zeal that God has given us.

Mr. Taylor says: "The zeal of the Apostles was seen in this—they preached publicly and privately; they prayed for all men; they wept to God for the hardness of men's hearts; they became all things to all men, that they might gain some; they traveled through deeps and deserts; they endured the heat of the Syrian sun and the violence of Euroclydon, winds and tempests, seas and prisons, mockings and scourgings, fastings and poverty, labor and watching; they endured of every man and wronged no man; they would do any good, and suffer any evil, if they could but hope to prevail upon a soul; they persuaded men meekly, they entreated them humbly, they convinced them powerfully; they watched for their good, but meddled not with their interest; and this is the Christian zeal—the zeal of meekness, the zeal of charity, the zeal of patience."

A good many people are afraid of the word Enthusiasm. Do you know what the word means? It means "In God." The person who is "in God", will surely be fired with enthusiasm. When a man goes into business filled with fire and zeal, he will generally carry all before him. In the army a general who is full of enthusiasm will fire up his men, and will accomplish a great deal more than one who is not stirred with the same spirit. People say that if we go on in that way many mistakes will be made. Probably there will. You never saw any boy learning a trade who did not make a good many mistakes. If you do not go to work because you are afraid of making mistakes, you will probably make one great mistake—the greatest mistake of your life—that of doing nothing. If we all do what we can, then a good deal will be accomplished.

How often do we find Sabbath-school teachers going into their work without any enthusiasm. I had just as soon have a lot of wooden teachers as some that I have known. If I were a carpenter I could manufacture any quantity of them. Take one of those teachers who has no heart, no fire, and no enthusiasm. He comes into the school-room perhaps a few minutes after the appointed time. He sits down, without speaking a word to any of the scholars, until the time comes for the lessons to begin. When the Superintendent says it is time to begin the teacher brings out a Question Book. He has not been at the trouble to look up the subject himself, so he gets what some one else has written about it. He takes care not only to get a Question Book, but an Answer Book.

Such a teacher will take up the first book and he says: "John, who was the first man?" (looking at the book)—"Yes, that is the right question." John replies, "Adam." Looking at the Answer Book the teacher says: "Yes, that is right." He looks again at the Question Book and he says: "Charles, who was Lot?" "Abraham's nephew." "Yes, my boy, that is right." And so he goes on. You may say that this is an exaggerated description, and of course I do not mean to say it is literally true; but the picture is not so much overdrawn as you would suppose. Do you think a class of little boys full of life and fire is going to be reached in that way?

I like to see a teacher come into the class and shake hands with the scholars all round. "Johnnie, how do you do? Charlie, I am glad to see you! How's the baby? How's your mother? How are all the folks at home?" That is the kind of a teacher I like to see. When he begins to open up the lesson all the scholars are interested in what he is going to say. He will be able to gain the attention of the whole class, and to train them for God and for eternity. You cannot find me a person in the world who has been greatly used of God, who has not been full of enthusiasm. When we enter on the work in this spirit it will begin to prosper, and God will give us success.

As I was leaving New York to go to England in 1867, a friend said to me: "I hope you will go to Edinburgh and be at the General Assembly this year. When I was there a year ago I heard such a speech as I shall never forget. Dr. Duff made a speech that set me all on fire. I shall never forget the hour I spent in that meeting." Shortly after reaching England I went to Edinburgh and spent a week there, in hopes that I might hear that one man speak. I went to work to find the report of the speech that my friend had referred to, and it stirred me wonderfully. Dr. Duff had been out in India as a missionary. He had spent twenty-five years there preaching the Gospel and establishing schools. He came back with a broken-down constitution. He was permitted to address the General Assembly, in order to make an appeal for men to go into the mission field. After he had spoken for a considerable time, he became exhausted and fainted away. They carried him out of the hall into another room. The doctors worked over him for some time, and at last he began to recover. When he realized where he was, he roused himself and said: "I did not finish my speech; carry me back and let me finish it." They told him he could only do it at the peril of his life. Said he: "I will do it if I die." So they took him back to the hall. My friend said it was one of the most solemn scenes he ever witnessed in his life.

They brought the white-haired man into the Assembly Hall, and as he appeared at the door every person sprang to his feet; the tears flowed freely as they looked upon the grand old veteran. With a trembling voice, he said: "Fathers and mothers of Scotland, is it true that you have no more sons to send to India to work for the Lord Jesus Christ? The call for help is growing louder and louder, but there are few coming forward to answer it. You have the money put away in the bank, but where are the laborers who shall go into the field? When Queen Victoria wants men to volunteer for her army in India, you freely give your sons. You do not talk about their losing their health, and about the trying climate. But when the Lord Jesus is calling for laborers, Scotland is saying: 'We have no more sons to give.'"

Turning to the President of the Assembly, he said: "Mr. Moderator, if it is true that Scotland has no more sons to give to the service of the Lord Jesus Christ in India; although I have lost my health in that land, if there are none who will go and tell those heathen of Christ, then I will be off to-morrow, to let them know that there is one old Scotchman who is ready to die for them. I will go back to the shores of the Ganges, and there lay down my life as a witness for the Son of God."

Thank God for such a man as that! We want men to-day who are willing, if need be, to lay down their lives for the Son of God. Then we shall be able to make an impression upon the world. When they see that we are in earnest, their hearts will be touched, and we shall be able to lead them to the Lord Jesus Christ.

I did not agree with Garibaldi's judgement in all things, but I must confess I did admire his enthusiasm. I never saw his name in the papers, or in a book, but I read all I could find about him. There was something about him that fired me up. I remember reading of the time when he was on the way to Rome in 1867, and when he was cast into prison. I read the letter he sent to his comrades: "If fifty Garibaldis are thrown into prison, let Rome be free!" He did not care for his own comfort, so long as the cause of freedom in Italy was advanced. If we have such a love for our Master and His cause that we are ready to go out and do His work whatever it may cost us personally, depend upon it the Lord will use us in building up His kingdom.

I have read of a man in the ninth century who came up against a king. The king had a force of thirty thousand men, and when he heard that this general had only five hundred men, he sent him a message that if he would surrender he would treat him and his followers mercifully. Turning to one of his followers, the man said: "Take that dagger and drive it to your heart." The man at once pressed the weapon to his bosom, and fell dead at the feet of his commander. Turning to another, he said: "Leap into yonder chasm." Into the jaws of death the man went; they saw him dashed to pieces at the bottom. Then turning to the king's messenger, the man said: "Go back to your king, and tell him that I have five hundred such men. Tell him that we may die but we never surrender. Tell him that I will have him chained with my dogs within forty-eight hours." When the king heard that he had such men arrayed against him, it struck terror to his heart. His forces were so demoralized that they were scattered like chaff before the wind. Within forty-eight hours the king was taken captive and chained with the dogs of his conqueror. When the people see that we are in earnest in all that we undertake for God, they will begin to tremble; men and women will be enquiring the way to Zion.

A fearful storm was raging, when the cry was heard, "Man overboard!" A human form was seen manfully breasting the furious elements in the direction of the shore; but the raging waves bore the struggler rapidly outward, and, ere the boats could be lowered, a fearful space separated the victim from help. Above the shriek of the storm and roar of the waters rose his rending cry. It was an agonizing moment. With bated breath and blanched cheek, every eye was strained to the struggling man. Manfully did the brave rowers strain every nerve in that race of mercy; but all their efforts were in vain. One wild shriek of despair, and the victim went down. A piercing cry, "Save him, save him!" rang through the hushed crowd; and into their midst darted an agitated man, throwing his arms wildly in the air, shouting, "A thousand pounds for the man who saves his life!" but his starting eye rested only on the spot where the waves rolled remorselessly over the perished. He whose strong cry broke the stillness of the crowd was Captain of the ship from whence the drowned man fell, and was his brother. This is the feeling we want to have in the various ranks of those bearing commission under the great Captain of our salvation. "Save him! he is my brother."

The fact is, men do not believe in Christianity because they think we are not in earnest about it. In this same Epistle to the Ephesians the Apostle says we are to be "living epistles of Christ, known and read of all men." I never knew a time when Christian people were ready to go forth and put in the sickle, but there was a great harvest. Wherever you put in the sickle you will find the fields white. The trouble is there are so few to reap.

God wants men and women; that is something far better than institutions. If a man or a woman be really in earnest, they will not wait to be put on some committee. If I saw a man fall into the river, and he was in danger of drowning, I would not wait until I was placed on some committee before I tried to save him. Many people say they cannot work because they have not been formally appointed. They say: "It is not my parish." I asked a person one day, during our last visit to London, if he would go and work in the inquiry room. The reply was: "I do not belong to this part of London." Let us look on the whole world as our parish, as a great harvest field. If God puts any one within our influence, let us tell them of Christ and heaven. The world may rise up and say that we are mad. In my opinion no one is fit for God's service until he is willing to be considered mad by the world. They said Paul was mad. I wish we had many more who were bitten with the same kind of madness. As some one has said: "If we are mad, we have a good Keeper on the way and a good Asylum at the end of the road."

One great trouble is that people come to special revival meetings, and for two or three weeks, perhaps, they will keep up the fire, but by and by it dies out. They are like a bundle of shavings with kerosene on the top—they blaze away for a little, but soon there is nothing left. We want to keep it all the time, morning, noon and night. I heard of a well once that was said to be very good, except that it had two faults. It would freeze up in the winter, and it would dry up in the summer. A most extraordinary well, but I am afraid there are many wells like it. There are many people who are good at certain times; as some one has expressed it, they seem to be good "in spots." What we want is to be red hot all the time. Do not wait till some one hunts you up. People talk about striking while the iron is hot. I believe it was Cromwell who said that he would rather strike the iron and make it hot. So let us keep at our post, and we will soon grow warm in the Lord's work.

Let me say a few words specially to Sabbath-school teachers. Let me urge upon you not to be satisfied with merely pointing the children away to the Lord Jesus Christ. There are so many teachers who go on sowing the seed, and who think they will reap the harvest by and by; but they do not look for the harvest now. I began to work in that way, and it was years before I saw any conversions. I believe God's method is that we should sow with one hand and reap with the other. The two should go on side by side. The idea that children must grow into manhood and womanhood before they can be brought to Jesus Christ is a false one. They can be led to Christ now in the days of their youth, and they can be kept, so that they may become useful members of society, and be a blessing to their parents, to the Church of God, and to the world. If they are allowed to grow up to manhood and womanhood before they are led to

Christ, many of them will be dragged into the dens of vice; and instead of being a blessing they will be a curse to society.

What is the trouble throughout Christendom to-day, in connection with the Sabbath-school? It is that so many when they grow up to the age of sixteen or so, drop through the Sabbath-school net, and that is the last we see of them. There are many young men now in our prisons who have been Sabbath scholars. The cause of that is that so few teachers believe the children can be converted when they are young. They do not labor to bring them to a knowledge of Christ, but are content to go on sowing the seed. Let a teacher resolve that, God helping him, he will not rest until he sees his whole class brought into the kingdom of God; if he thus resolves he will see signs and wonders inside of thirty days.

I well remember how I got waked up on this point. I had a large Sunday-school with a thousand children. I was very much pleased with the numbers. If they only kept up or exceeded that number I was delighted; if the attendance fell below a thousand I was very much troubled. I was all the time aiming simply at numbers. There was one class held in a corner of the large hall. It was made up of young women, and it was more trouble than any other in the school. There was but one man who could ever manage it and keep it in order. If he could manage to keep the class quiet I thought it was about as much as we could hope for. The idea of any of them being converted never entered my mind.

One Sabbath this teacher was missing, and it was with difficulty that his substitute could keep order in the class. During the week the teacher came to my place of business. I noticed that he looked very pale, and I asked what was the trouble. "I have been bleeding at the lungs," he said, "and the doctor tells me I cannot live. I must give up my class and go back to my widowed mother in New York State." He fully believed he was going home to die. As he spoke to me his chin quivered, and the tears began to flow. I noticed this and said: "You are not afraid of death, are you?" "Oh, no, I am not afraid to die, but I will meet God, and not one of my Sabbath-school scholars is converted. What shall I say?" Ah, how different things looked when he felt he was going to render an account of his stewardship.

I was speechless. It was something new to me to hear any one speak in that way. I said: "Suppose we go and see the scholars and tell them about Christ." "I am very weak," he said, "too weak to walk." I said I would take him in a carriage. We took a carriage and went round to the residence of every scholar. He would just be able to stagger across the sidewalk, sometimes leaning on my arm. Calling the young lady by name, he would pray with her and plead with her to come to Christ. It was a new experience for me. I got a new view of things. After he had used up all his strength I would take him home. Next day he would start again and visit others in the class. Sometimes he would go alone, and sometimes I would go with him. At the end of ten days he came to my place of business, his face beaming with joy, and said: "The last one has yielded her heart to Christ. I am going home now; I have done all I can do; my work is done."

I asked when he was going, and he said: "To-morrow night." I said: "Suppose I ask these young friends to have a little gathering, to meet you once more before you go." He said he would be very glad. I sent out the invitations and they all came together. I had never spent such a night up to that time. I had never met such a large number of young converts, led to Christ by his influence and mine. We prayed for each member of the class, for the Superintendent, and for the teacher. Every one of them prayed; what a change had come over them in a short space of time. We tried to sing—but we did not get on very well—

> "Blest be the tie that binds
> Our hearts in Christian love."

We all bade him good-bye; but I felt as if I must go and see him once more. Next night, before the train started, I went to the station, and found that, without any concert of action, one and another of the class had come to bid him good-bye. They were all there on the platform. A few gathered around us—the fireman, engineer, brakesman, and conductor of the train, with the passengers. It was a beautiful summer night, and the sun was just going down behind the western prairies as we sang together—

> "Here we meet to part again,
> But when we meet on Canaan's shore,
> There'll be no parting there."

As the train moved out of the station, he stood on the outside platform, and, with his finger pointing heavenward, he said: "I will meet you yonder;" then he disappeared from our view.

What a work was accomplished in those ten days! Some of the members of that class were among the most active Christians we had in the school for years after. Some of them are active workers to-day. I met one of them at work away out on the Pacific Coast, a few years ago. We had a blessed work of grace in the school that summer; it took me out of my business and sent me into the Lord's work. If it had not been for the work of those ten days, probably I should not have been an evangelist to-day.

Let me again urge on Sunday-school teachers to seek the salvation of your scholars. Make up your mind that within the next ten days you will do all you can to lead your class to Christ. Fathers, mothers, let there be no rest till you see all your family brought into the kingdom of God. Do you say that He will not bless such consecrated effort? What we want to-day is the spirit of consecration and concentration. May God pour out His Spirit upon us, and fill us with a holy enthusiasm.

CHAPTER VI

THE POWER OF LITTLE THINGS

In the twenty-fifth chapter of Exodus we read: "And the Lord spake unto Moses, saying: 'Speak unto the children of Israel, that they bring Me an offering: of every man that giveth it willingly with his heart ye shall take my offering. And this is the offering which ye shall take of them: gold, and silver, and brass, and blue, and purple, and scarlet, and fine linen, and goats' hair, and rams' skins dyed red, and badgers' skins, and shittim wood, oil for the light, spices for anointing oil and for sweet incense, onyx stones, and stones to be set in the ephod and in the breastplate. And let them make Me a sanctuary; that I may dwell among them. According to all that I show thee, after the pattern of the tabernacle, and the pattern of all the instruments thereof, even so shall ye make it.'"

I am glad this has been recorded for our instruction. How it ought to encourage us all to believe that we may each have a part in building up the walls of the heavenly Zion. In all ages God has delighted to use the weak things. In his letter to the Corinthians Paul speaks of five things that God uses: "God hath chosen the foolish things of the world to confound the wise; and God hath chosen the weak things of the world to confound the things which are mighty; and base things of the world, and things which are despised, hath God chosen, yea, and things which are not, to bring to nought things that are, that no flesh should glory in His presence."

You notice there are five things mentioned that God uses—foolish things, weak things, base things, despised things, and things which are not. What for? "That no flesh should glory in His presence." When we are weak then we are strong. People often think they have not strength enough; the fact is we have too much strength. It is when we feel that we have no strength of our own, that we are willing God should use us, and work through us. If we are leaning on God's strength, we have more than all the strength of the world.

This world is not going to be reached by mere human intellectual power. When we realize that we have no strength, then all the fulness of God will flow in upon us. Then we shall have power with God and with man.

In Revelation we read that John on one occasion wept much at a sight he beheld in heaven. He saw a sealed book; and no one was found that could break the seal and open the book. Abel, that holy man of God, was not worthy to open it. Enoch, who had been translated to heaven without tasting death; Elijah, who had gone up in a chariot of fire; even Moses, that great law-giver; or Isaiah, or any of the prophets—none was found worthy to open the book. As he saw this John wept much. As he wept one touched him, and said: "Weep not; behold, the Lion of the tribe of Judah, the root of David, hath prevailed to open the Book, and to loose the seven seals thereof." When he looked to see who was the Lion of the tribe of Judah, whom did he see! Lo, the Lion was a Lamb! God's Lion is a Lamb! When we are like lambs God can use us, and we are strong in His service. We can all be weak can we not? Then let us lean on the mighty power of God.

Notice that all the men whom Christ called around Him were weak men in a worldly sense. They were all men without rank, without title, without position, without wealth or culture. Nearly all of them were fishermen and unlettered men; yet Christ chose them to build up His kingdom. When God wanted to bring the children of Israel out of bondage, He did not send an army; He sent one solitary man. So in all ages God has used the weak things of the world to accomplish His purposes.

I read an incident some time ago that illustrates the power of a simple tract. A society was some years ago established to distribute tracts by mail in the higher circles. One of these tracts, entitled, "Prepare to meet thy God," was enclosed in an envelope, and sent by post to a gentleman well known for his ungodly life and his reckless impiety. He was in his study when he read this letter among others. "What's that," said he. "'Prepare to meet thy God.' Who has had the impudence to send me this cant?" And, with an imprecation on his unknown correspondent, he arose to put the paper in the fire.

"No; I won't do that." he said to himself; "On second thoughts, I know what I will do. I'll send it to my friend B—; it will be a good joke to hear what he'll say about it." So saying, he enclosed the tract in a fresh envelope, and, in a feigned hand, directed it to his boon companion.

Mr. B— was a man of his own stamp, and received the tract, as his friend had done, with an oath at the Methodistical humbug, which his first impulse was to tear in pieces. "I'll not tear it either," said he to himself. "Prepare to meet thy God" at once arrested his attention, and smote his conscience. The arrow of conviction entered his heart as he read, and he was converted. Almost his first thought was for his ungodly associates. "Have I received such blessed light and truth, and shall I not strive to communicate it to others?" He again folded the tract, and enclosed and directed it to one of his companions in sin. Wonderful to say, the little arrow hit the mark. His friend read. He also was converted; and both are now walking as the Lord's redeemed ones.

In Matthew we read: "For the kingdom of heaven is as a man

travelling into a far country, who called his own servants, and delivered unto them his goods. And unto one he gave five talents, to another two, and to another one; to every man according to his several ability; and straightway took his journey."

Observe, he gave to every man "according to his several ability." He gave to each servant just the number of talents that he could take care of and use. Some people complain that they have not more talents; but we have each the number of talents that we can properly employ. If we take good care of what we have, God will give us more. There were eight talents to be distributed among three persons; the master gave to one five; to a second, two; and to another, one. The man went away; and the servants fully understood that he expected them to improve their talents and trade with them. God is not unreasonable; He does not ask us to do what we cannot do; but He gives us according to our several ability, and He expects us to use the talents we have.

We read: "He that had received the five talents went and traded with the same, and made them other five talents. And likewise he that had received two, he also gained other two. But he that had received one went and digged in the earth, and hid his lord's money." Notice that the man who had the two talents got exactly the same commendation as the man who had the five. The one who got five doubled them, and his lord said to him: "Well done, good and faithful servant." The one who had two also doubled them, and so had four talents; to him also the lord said: "Well done, good and faithful servant, enter thou into the joy of thy lord."

If the man who had the one talent had traded with it, he would have received exactly the same approval as the others. But what did he do? He put it into a napkin and buried it. He thought he would take care of it in that way.

After the lord of these servants had been gone a long while he returned to reckon with them. What does he find in the case of the third servant? He has the one talent; but that is all.

I read of a man who had a thousand dollars. He hid it away, thinking he would in that way take care of it, and that when he was an old man he would have something to fall back upon. After keeping the money for twenty years he took it to a bank and got just one thousand dollars for it. If he had put it at interest, in the usual way, he might have had three times the amount. He made the mistake that a great many people are making to-day throughout Christendom, of not trading with his talents. My experience has been as I have gone about in the world and mingled with professing Christians, that those who find most fault with others are those who themselves have nothing to do. If a person is busy improving the talents that God has given him he will have too much to do to find fault and complain about others.

God has given us many opportunities of serving Him, and He expects that we should use them. People think that their time and property are their own. What saying is more frequent than this? "I have a right to do what I will with my own."

On one occasion a friend was beside the dying bed of a military man who had held an important command in successful Indian wars. He asked if he were afraid to die. He at once said: "I am not."

"Why?" He said: "I have never done any harm."

The other replied: "If you were going to be tried by a court-martial as an officer and a gentleman, I suppose you would expect an honorable acquittal?" The dying old man lifted himself up, and with an energy which his illness seemed to render impossible, exclaimed, "That I should!"

"But you are not going to a court-martial; you are going to Christ; and when Christ asks you, 'What have you done for me?' what will you say?" His countenance changed, and earnestly gazing on his friend, with agonized feelings he answered: "Nothing!—I have never done anything for Christ!"

His friend pointed out the awful mistake of habitually living in the sense of our relations one with another, and forgetting our relation to Christ and to God; therefore the error of supposing that doing no harm, or even doing good to those around, will serve as a substitute for living to God. What have you done for Christ? is the great question.

After some days, he called again on the old man, who said: "Well, sir, what do you think now?" He replied: "Ah! I am a poor sinner." He pointed him to the Savior of sinners; and not long afterward he departed this life as a repentant sinner, resting in Christ. What an awful end would have come to the false peace in which he was found! And yet it is the peace of the multitudes, only to be undeceived at the judgment seat of Christ.

If this world is going to be reached, I am convinced it must be done by men and women of average talent. After all there are comparatively few people in the world who have great talents. Here is a man with one talent; there is another with three; perhaps I may have only half a talent. But if we all go to work and trade with the gifts we have the Lord will prosper us; and we may double or treble our talents. What we need is to be up and about our Master's work, every man building against his own house. The more we use the means and opportunities we have, the more will our ability and our opportunities be increased.

An Eastern allegory runs thus: A merchant, going abroad for a time, gave respectively to two of his friends two sacks of wheat each, to take care of against his return. Years passed; he came back, and applied for them again. The first took him into a storehouse, and showed them his sacks; but they were mildewed and worthless. The other led him out into the open country, and pointed to field after field of waving corn, the produce of the two sacks given him. Said the merchant: "You have been a faithful friend. Give me two sacks of that wheat; the rest shall be thine."

I heard a person once say that she wanted assurance. I asked how long she had been a Christian; and she replied she had been one for a number of years. I said: "What are you doing for Christ?" "I do not know that I have the opportunity of doing anything," she replied. I pity the person who professes to be a Christian in this day, and who says he can find no opportunities of doing any work for Christ. I cannot imagine where his lot must be cast. The idea of any one knowing the Lord Jesus Christ in this nineteenth century, and saying he has no opportunities of testifying for Him. Surely no one need look far to find plenty of opportunities for speaking and working for the Master, if he only has the desire to do it. "Lift up your eyes, and look on the fields; for they are white already to harvest." If you cannot do some great thing, you can do some little thing.

A man sent me a tract a little while ago, entitled, "What is that in thine hand?" and I am very thankful he sent it. These words were spoken by God to Moses when He called him to go down to Egypt, and bring the children of Israel out of the house of bondage. You remember how Moses tried to excuse himself. He said he was not eloquent; he was not this and that; and he could not go. Like Isaiah he wanted the Lord to send some one else. At last the Lord said to Moses, "What is that in thine hand?" He had a rod in his hand. It may be that a few days before he wanted something to drive the sheep with, and he may have cut this wand for that purpose. He could probably have got a hundred better rods any day. Yet with that he was to deliver the children of Israel. God was to link His almighty power with that rod; and that was enough.

I can imagine that as Moses was on his way down to Egypt he may have met one of the philosophers or free-thinkers of his day, who might have asked him where he was going. "Down to Egypt." "Indeed! are you going down there again to live?" "No, I am going to bring my people out of the house of bondage." "What! you are going to deliver them from the hand of Pharaoh, the mightiest monarch now living? You think you are going to free three millions of slaves from the power of the Egyptians?" "Yes."

"How are you going to do it?" "With this rod."

What a contemptible thing the rod must have been in the eyes of that Egyptian freethinker; the idea of delivering three millions of slaves with a rod! We had three millions of slaves in this country, and before they could be set free half a million of men had to lay down their lives. The flower of the nation marched to its grave before our slaves gained their deliverance.

Here was a weak and solitary man going down to Egypt, to meet a monarch who had the power of life and death. And all he had with which to deliver the people from bondage was this rod! Yet see how famous that rod became. When Moses wanted to bring up the plagues on the people he had only to stretch out his rod, and they covered the land. He had but to stretch it out, and the water of the country was turned into blood. Then when the people came to the Red Sea and they wanted to go across, he had only to lift up the rod and the waters separated, so that the people could pass through dry-shod. When they were in the desert and wanted water to drink, again he lifted this rod and struck the flinty rock, when the water burst forth, and they drank and were refreshed. That contemptible rod became mighty indeed. But it was not the rod; it was the God of Moses, who condescended to use it.

Let us learn a lesson from this history. We are required to use what we have, not what we have not. Whatever gifts or talents you have, take and lay them at the Master's feet. Moses took what he had; and we see how much he accomplished. If we are ready to say: "Here am I, ready and willing to be used," the Lord will use us; He will link His mighty power with our weakness, and we shall be able to do great things for Him.

Look again, and see Joshua as he goes up to the walls of Jericho. If you had asked what they had with which to bring down the walls of that city, all you would have seen would have been a few rams' horns. They must have looked very mean and contemptible in the eyes of the men of Jericho. Perhaps the city contained some men who were giants; as they looked over the walls and saw the Israelites marching around the city blowing these horns, they must have appeared very insignificant. But God can use the base things, the despised things. However contemptible an instrument a ram's horn may have appeared in the sight of man, the people went on blowing them as they were commanded; and at the appointed time down came the walls, and the city was taken. The Israelites had no battering rams; no great armor or mighty weapons of any kind. They simply took what they had, and God used it to do the work.

Look at Samson going out to meet a thousand Philistines. What has he with him? Only the jawbone of an ass! If God could use that, surely He can use us, can he not? Do you tell me He cannot use this woman, that little boy? There is not one whom He cannot use, if we are willing to be used.

I remember hearing a Scotchman say, when I was in Great Britain ten years ago, that there was probably not a man in all Saul's army but believed that God could use him to go out and slay the giant of Gath. But there was only one solitary man who believed that God would use him. David went out to meet Goliath and we know the result. We all believe that God can use us; we want to take a step further and believe that He will use us. If we are willing to be used, He is willing to use us in His service. How contemptible these smooth stones that David took out of the brook would have appeared to Goliath! Even Saul wanted David to take his armor, and put it on. He was on the point of yielding; but he took his sling and the five smooth stones and went out. The giant of Gath fell before him. Let us go forth in the name of the God of hosts, using what we have, and He will give us the victory.

When I was in Glasgow a few years ago, a friend was telling me about an open-air preacher who died there some years before. This man was preaching one Sabbath morning on Shamgar. He said: "I can imagine that when he was ploughing in the field a man came running over the hill all out of breath, and shouted: 'Shamgar! Shamgar! There are six hundred Philistines coming toward you.' Shamgar quietly said: 'You pass on; I can take care of them, they are four hundred short.' So he took an ox goad and slew the whole of them. He routed them hip and high. And the Israelites had again fulfilled before their eyes the words: 'One shall chase a thousand and two shall put ten thousand to flight.'" Now-a-days it takes about a thousand to chase one, because we do not realize that we are weak in ourselves and that our strength is in God.

We want to remember that it is true to-day as ever it was that "One shall chase a thousand." What we need is Holy Ghost power that can take up the weakest child here and make him mighty in God's hand. There is a mountain to be threshed; there lies a bar of iron, and a little weak worm. God puts aside the iron, and takes up the worm to thresh the mountain. That is God's way. His thoughts are not our thoughts; His plans are not ours.

We say: "If such and such a man were only converted—that rich man or that wealthy lady—how much good would be done!" Very true; but it may be that God will pass them by and take up some poor tramp, and make him the greatest instrument for good in all the land. John Bunyan, the poor Bedford tinker, was worth more than all the nobility of his day. God took him in hand, and he became mighty. He wrote that wonderful book that has gone marching through the nations, lifting up many a weary heart, cheering many a discouraged and disheartened one. Let us remember that if we are willing to be used, God is willing and waiting to use us.

I once heard an Englishman speak about Christ feeding the five thousand with the five barley loaves and the two small fishes. He said that Christ may have taken one of the loaves and broken off a piece and given it to one of the disciples to divide. When the disciple began to pass it round he only gave a very small piece to the first, because he was afraid it would not hold out. But after he had given the first piece it did not seem to grow any the less; so the next time he gave a larger piece, and still the bread was not exhausted. The more he gave, the more the bread increased, until all had plenty.

At the first all could be carried in one basket; but when the whole multitude had been satisfied the disciples gathered up twelve baskets full of fragments. They had a good deal more when they stopped than when they began. Let us bring our little barley loaves to the Master that He may multiply them.

You say you have not got much; well, you can use what you have. The longer I work in Christ's vineyard the more convinced I am that a good many are kept out of the service of Christ, deprived of the luxury of working for God, because they are trying to do some great thing. Let us be willing to do little things. And let us remember that nothing is small in which God is. Elijah's servant came to him and told him he saw a cloud not larger than a man's hand. That was enough for Elijah. He said to his servant, "Go, tell Ahab to make haste; there is the sound of abundance of rain." Elijah knew that the small cloud would bring rain. Nothing that we do for God is small.

I remember holding meetings some years ago at a certain place, and I met a young lady at the house where I was staying. She told me she had a Sunday afternoon class in a mission-school. At one of our afternoon meetings I saw this lady sitting right in front; she must have been there early to get a good seat. After the service I met her, and I said: "I saw you at the meeting to-day; I thought you had a class." "So I have."

"Did you get some one to take it for you?" "No."

"Did you tell the Superintendent you were not to be there?" "No."

"Do you know who had the class?" "No."

"Do you know if any one was there to take it?" "I am afraid there was nobody; for I saw a good many of the teachers of the school at your meeting."

"Is that the way you do the Lord's work?" "Well, you know, I have only five little boys. I thought it would not make any difference."

Only five little boys! Why, there might have been a John Knox, or a

Wesley, or a Whitefield, or a Bunyan there. You cannot tell what these boys might become. One of them might become another Martin Luther; there might be a second Reformation slumbering in one of these five little boys. It is a great thing for any one to take "five little boys" and train them for God and for eternity. You may set a stream in motion that will flow on after you are dead and gone.

Little did the mothers of the Wesleys know what would be the result, when she trained her boys for God and for His kingdom. See what mighty results have flowed from that one source. It is estimated that there are to-day 25,000,000 adherents of the Methodist faith, and over 5,000,000 communicants. It is estimated there are 110,000 regular and local preachers in the United States alone. Two new churches are being built every day in the year; and the work of the Methodist Church is spreading over this great Republic. And all this has been done in about a hundred and fifty years. Let not mothers think that their work of training children for God is a small one. In the sight of God it is very great; many may rise up in eternity to call them blessed.

I have now in my mind a mother who has had twelve boys. They have all grown up to be active Christians. A number of them are preachers of the Gospel; and all of them are true to the Son of God. There are very few women in our country who have done more for the nation than that mother. It is a great thing to be permitted to touch God's work, and to be a co-worker with Him.

There is a bridge over the Niagara River. It is one of the great highways of the nation; trains pass over it every few minutes of the day. When they began to make the bridge, the first thing they did was to take a boy's kite and send a little thread across the stream. It seemed a very small thing, but it was the beginning of a great work. So if we only lead one soul to Christ, eternity alone may tell what the result will be. You may be the means of saving some one who may become one of the most eminent men in the service of God that the world has ever seen.

We may not be able to do any great thing; but if each of us will do something, however small it may be, a goof deal will be accomplished for God. For a good many years I have made it a rule not to let any day pass without speaking to some one about eternal things. I commenced it away back years ago, and if I live the life allotted to man, there will be 18,250 persons who will have been spoken to personally by me. That of course does not take into account those to whom I speak publicly. How often we as Christians meet with people, when we might turn the conversation into a channel that will lead them up to Christ.

There are many burdened hearts all around us; can we not help to remove these burdens? Some one has represented this world as two great mountains—a mountain of sorrow and a mountain of joy. If we can each day take something from the mountain of sorrow and add it to the mountain of joy, a good deal will be accomplished in the course of a year.

I remember Mr. Spurgeon making this remark a few days ago: When Moses went to tell the king of Egypt that he would call up the plague of frogs upon the land, the king may have said: "Your God is the God of frogs, is He? I am not afraid of them; bring them on, I do not care for the frogs!" Says Moses: "But there are a good many of them, O king." And he found that out.

So we may be weak and contemptible individually, but there a good many Christians scattered all over the land, and we can accomplish a great deal between us. Supposing each one who loves the Lord Jesus were to resolve to-day, by God's help, to try and lead one soul to Christ this week. Is there a professing Christian who cannot lead some soul into the kingdom of God? If you cannot I want to tell you that there is something wrong in your life; you had better have it straightened out at once. If you have not an influence for good over some one of your friends or neighbors, there is something in your life that needs to be put right. May God show it to you to-day!

I have little sympathy with the idea that a Christian man or woman has to live for years before they can have the privilege of leading anyone out of the darkness of this world into the kingdom of God. I do not believe, either, that all God's work is going to be done by ministers, and other officers in the Churches. This lost world will never be reached and brought back to loyalty to God, until the children of God wake up to the fact that they have a mission in the world. If we are true Christians we should all be missionaries. Christ came down from heaven on a mission, and if we have His Spirit in us we will be missionaries too. If we have no desire to see the world discipled, to see man brought back to God, there is something very far wrong in our religion.

If you cannot work among the elder people you can go to work among the children. Let Christians speak kindly to these boys and girls about their souls; they will remember it all their lives. They may forget the sermon, but if some one speaks to them personally, they will say: "That man or woman must be greatly interested in me or they would not have been at the trouble to speak to me." They may wake up to the fact that they have immortal souls, and even if the preaching goes right over their heads, a little personal effort may be a means of blessing to them.

This personal and individual dealing is perfectly Scriptural. Philip was called away from a great work in Samaria to go and speak to one man in the desert. Christ's great sermon on Regeneration was addressed to one man; and that wonderful discourse by our Lord on the Water of Life was spoken to one poor sinful woman. I pity those Christians who are not willing to speak to one soul; they are not fit for God's service. We shall not accomplish much for God in the world, if we are not willing to speak to the ones and twos.

Another thing: Do not let Satan make you believe that the children are too young to be saved. Of course you cannot put old heads on young shoulders. You cannot make them into deacons and elders all at once. But they can give their young hearts to Christ.

A good many years ago I had a mission school in Chicago. The children were mostly those of ungodly parents. I only had them about an hour out of the week, and it seemed as if any good they got was wiped out during the week. I used to think that if ever I became a public speaker I would go up and down the world and beseech parents to consider the importance of training their children for God and eternity. On one of the first Sabbaths I went out of Chicago I impressed this on the congregation.

When I had finished my address an old white-haired man got up. I was all in a tremble, thinking he was going to criticise what I had said. Instead of that he said: "I want to indorse all that this young man has spoken. Sixteen years ago I was in a heathen country. My wife died and left me with three motherless children. The first Sabbath after her death my eldest girl, ten years old, said: 'Papa, may I take the children into the bedroom and pray with them as mother used to do on the Sabbath?' I said she might.

When they came out of the room after a time I saw that my eldest daughter had been weeping. I called her to me, and said: 'Nellie, what is the trouble?' 'Oh, father,' she said, 'after we went into the room I made the prayer that mother taught me to make.' Then, naming her little brother, He made the prayer that mother taught him. Little Susie didn't use to pray when mother took us in there because mother thought she was too young. But when we got through she made a prayer of her own. I could not but weep when I heard her pray. She put her little hands together and closed her eyes and said: 'O God, you have taken away my dear mamma, and I have no mamma now to pray for me. Won't you bless me and make me good just as mamma was, for Jesus Christ's sake, Amen.'" "Little Susie gave evidence of having given her young heart to God before she was four years old. For sixteen years she has been at work as a missionary among the heathen."

Let us remember that God can use these little children. Dr. Milnor was brought up a Quaker, became a distinguished lawyer in Philadelphia, and was a member of Congress for three successive terms. Returning to his home on a visit during his last

Congressional session, his little daughter rushed upon him exclaiming. "Papa! papa! do you know I can read?" "No?" he said, "let me hear you!" She opened her little Bible and read, "Thou shalt love the Lord thy God with all thy heart." It was an arrow in her father's heart, It came to him as a solemn admonition. "Out of the mouth of babes," God's Spirit moved within him. He was driven to his closet, and a friend calling upon him found he had been weeping over the Dairyman's Daughter. Although only forty years of age, he abandoned politics and law for the ministry of the Gospel. For thirty years he was the beloved rector of St. George's Church, in Philadelphia, the predecessor of the venerated Dr. Tyng.

Dear mothers and fathers, let us in simple faith bring our children to Christ. He is the same to-day as when He took them in His arms and said: "Suffer the little children to come unto Me and forbid them not; for of such is the kingdom of heaven."

> I may not do much with all my care,
> But I surely may bless a few;
> The loving Jesus will give to me,
> Some work of love to do;
> I may wipe the tears from some weeping eyes,
> I may bring the smile again
> To a face that is weary and worn with care,
> To a heart that is full of pain.
> I may speak His name to the sorrowful,
> As I journey by their side;
> To the sinful and despairing ones
> I may preach of the Crucified.
> I may drop some little gentle word
> In the midst of some scene of strife;
> I may comfort the sick and the dying
> With a thought of eternal life.
>
> Marianne Farningham

CHAPTER VII

"SHE HATH DONE WHAT SHE COULD"

In the gospel by Mark we read: "After two days was the feast of the Passover, and of unleavened bread: and the Chief Priests and the Scribes sought how they might take Him by craft, and put Him to death. But they said, not on the feast day, lest there be an uproar of the people. And being in Bethany in the house of Simon the leper, as He sat at meat, there came a woman having an alabaster box of ointment of spikenard, very precious; and she brake the box, and poured it on His head. And there were some that had indignation within themselves, and said, Why was this waste of the ointment made? For it might have been sold for more than three hundred pence, and have been given to the poor. And they murmured against her. And Jesus said, 'Let her alone; why trouble ye her? She hath wrought a good work for Me. For ye have the poor with you always, and whensoever ye will ye may do them good; but Me ye have not always. She hath done what she could; she is come aforehand to anoint My body to the burying. Verily I say unto you, wheresoever this Gospel shall be preached throughout the whole world, this also that she hath done shall be spoken of for a memorial of her.'"

John tells us in his Gospel who this woman was. "Then Jesus six days before the Passover came to Bethany, where Lazarus was which had been dead, whom He raised from the dead. There they made Him a supper, and Martha served; but Lazarus was one of them that sat at the table with him. Then took Mary a pound of ointment of spikenard, very costly, and anointed the feet of Jesus, and wiped his feet with her hair; and the house was filled with the odor of the ointment. Then saith one of His disciples, Judas Iscariot, Simon's son, which should betray Him: 'Why was not this ointment sold for three hundred pence, and given to the poor?' This he said, not that he cared for the poor; but because he was a thief, and had the bag, and bare what was put therein. Then said Jesus, 'Let her alone: against the day of My burying hath she kept this. For the poor always ye have with you; but Me ye have not always.'"

This is the last time we have a glimpse of the family at Bethany. It was Christ's last week there, and here we have the last recorded interview between Christ and that lovely family.

Speaking of Martha and Mary some one has said: "They were both dear to Jesus and they both loved Him, but they were different. The eye of one saw His weariness and would give to Him; the faith of the other apprehended His fulness and would draw from Him; Martha's service was acceptable to the Lord and was acknowledged by Him, but He would not allow it to disturb Mary's communion. Mary knew his mind; she had deeper fellowship with Him; her heart clung to Himself."

I want to call your attention specially to one clause from this fourteenth chapter of Mark, "She hath done what she could." If some one had reported in Jerusalem that something was going to happen at Bethany on that memorable day, that should outlive the Roman Empire, and all the monarchs that had ever existed or would exist, there would have been great excitement in the city. A good many people would have gone down to Bethany that day to see the thing that was going to happen, and that was to live so long. Little did Mary think that she was going to erect a monument which would outlive empires and kingdoms. She never thought of herself. Love does not think of itself. What does Christ say: "Wheresoever this Gospel shall be preached throughout the whole world, this also that she hath done shall be spoken of for a memorial of her."

This one story has already been put into three hundred and fifty different languages, and it is now in circulation in every nation under heaven. Day by day this story is being printed and published. One society in London alone prints, every working hour of the day, five hundred records of this act that took place at Bethany. It is being spread abroad in all the corners of the earth. It will be told out as long as the Church of God exists. Matthew speaks of it; so does John; and so does Mark.

Men seek to erect some monument that will live after they are dead and gone. This woman never thought to erect a monument; she simply wanted to lavish her love upon Christ. But the act has lived and will continue to live while the Church is on earth. It is as fresh to-day as it was a hundred years ago: it is fresher than it was five hundred years ago. In fact there never was a time when it was so well known as to-day. Although Mary was herself unknown outside of Bethany when she performed the act, now it is known over all the world. Kings have come and gone; empires have risen and crumbled. Egypt, with its ancient glories, has passed away. Greece, with its wise men and its mighty philosophers and its warriors, has been almost forgotten. The great Roman empire has passed away. We do not know the names of those who are buried in the Pyramids, or of those who were embalmed in Egypt, with so much care and trouble, but the record of this humble life continues to be an inspiration to others.

Here is a woman whose memory has outlived Cæsar, Alexander, Cyrus, and all the great warriors of the ancient world. We do not know that she was wealthy, or beautiful, or gifted, or great in the eye of the world. What we do know is that she loved the Savior. She took this box of precious ointment and broke it over the body of Christ. Some one has said it was the only thing He ever received that He did not give away. It was a small thing in the sight of the world. If there had been daily papers in those days, and some Jerusalem reporter had been looking out for items of news that would interest the inhabitants, I suppose he would not have thought it worth putting into his paper. Yet it has outlived all that happened in that century, except, of course, the sayings, and the other events connected with the life of Christ. Mary had Christ in her heart as well as in her creed. She loved Him and she showed her love in acts.

Thank God, everyone of us can love Christ, and we can all do something for Him. It may be a small thing; but whatever it is it shall be lasting; it will outlive all the monuments on earth. The iron and the granite will rust and crumble and fade away, but anything done for Christ will never fade. It will be more lasting than time itself. Christ says: "Heaven and earth shall pass away, but My word shall not pass away."

Look again and see that woman in the temple. Christ stood there as the people passed by and cast their offerings into the treasury. The widow had but two mites and she cast it all in. The Lord saw that her heart was in it, and so He commended her. If some nobleman had cast in a thousand dollars Christ would probably not have noticed it, unless his heart had gone with it. Gold is of little value in heaven. It is so plentiful there that they use it to pave the streets with; and it is transparent gold, much better gold than we have in this world. It is when the heart goes with the offering that it is accepted of Christ. So He said of this woman: "She hath cast in more than they all." She had done all she could.

I think this is the lesson we are to learn from these Scripture incidents. The Lord expects us to do what we can. We can all do something. In one of our Southern cities a few Christian people gathered together at the beginning of the war to see what could be done about building a church in a part of the city where the poor were very much neglected. After they had discussed the matter they wanted to see how much could be raised out of the congregation.

One said he would give so much; others said they would give so much. They only got about half the amount that was needed, and it was thought they would have to abandon the project. Away back in the meeting there sat a washerwoman. She rose and said her little boy had died a week before. All he had was a gold dollar. She said: "It is all I have, but I will give the dollar to the cause." Her words touched the hearts of many of those who heard them. Rich men were ashamed at what they had given. The whole sum was raised within a very short time. I have spoken in that church, and I know it to be a centre of influence in one of our great cities. This poor woman did what she could; perhaps she gave more in proportion than anyone in the city.

When we were in London eight years ago, we wanted the city to be canvassed; we called for volunteers to go and visit the people in their own homes and invite them to come to the meetings. Among those who came forward was an old woman, eighty-five years of age. She said she wanted to do a little more for the Master before she went home. She took a district and went from house to house, delivering the messages of invitation and the tracts to the people. I suppose she has now gone to her reward, but I shall never forget her. She wanted to do what she could. If every Christian man and woman will do what Mary did, multitudes will be reached and blessed.

Years ago, when Illinois was but a young State, there were only a few settlers here and there throughout a large portion. One of these was a man who used to spend his Sundays in hunting and fishing. He was a profane and notoriously wicked man. His little girl went to the Sabbath-school at the log school-house. There she was taught the way into the kingdom of God. When she was converted the teacher tried to tell her how she might be used of God in doing good to others. She thought she would begin with her father. Others had tried to reach him and had failed to do it, but his own child had more influence with him. It is written, "A little child shall lead them." She got him to promise to go to the meeting. He came to the door, but at first he would not go in. He had gone to the school when he was young, but one day the boys laughed at him because he had a little impediment in his speech. He would not go back, and so he had never learned to read.

However he was at last induced to go to the Sabbath-school. There he heard of Christ, and he was converted to God. His little child helped him and others helped him, and he soon learned to read. This man has since been called to his reward, but about two years ago when I saw him last, if I remember well, that man had established on the Western prairies between 1,100 and 1,200 Sunday-schools. In addition to all these school-houses, scattered about over the country, churches have sprung up. There are now hundreds of flourishing churches that have grown out of these little mission schools that he planted. He used to have a Sunday-school horse, a "Robert Raikes" horse he called him, on which he traveled up and down the country, going into many outlying districts where nothing was being done for Christ. He used to gather the parents into the log school-houses and tell how his little girl led him to Christ. I have heard a great many orators, but I never heard any who could move an audience as he could. There was no impediment in his speech when he began to speak for Christ; he seemed to have all the eloquence and fire of heaven. That little girl did what she could. She did a good day's work when she led her father to the Savior.

Every one of us may do something. If we are only willing to do what we can, the Lord will condescend to use us; and it will be a great thing to be instruments in His hand that He may do with us what He will.

I remember reading in the papers that when the theatre in Vienna was on fire a few years ago, a man in one of the corridors was hurrying out. Many others of the people were trying to find their way out so as to escape from the fire. It was dark, but this man had a single match in his pocket. He struck it, and by doing so he was able to save twenty lives. He did what he could.

You think you cannot do much. If you are the means of saving one soul, he may be instrumental in saving a hundred more. I remember when we were in England ten years ago, there was a woman in the city where we labored who got stirred up. I do not know but it was this very text that moved her, "She hath done what she could." She had been a nominal Christian for a good many years, but she had not thought that she had any particular mission in the world. I am afraid that is the condition of many professedly Christian men and women. Now she began to look about her to see what she could do. She thought she would try and do something for her fallen sisters in that town. She went out and began to talk kindly to those she met on the street. She hired a house and invited them to come and meet her there.

When we went back to that city about a year or so ago, she had rescued over three hundred of these fallen ones, and had restored them to their parents and homes. She is now corresponding with many of them. Think of more than three hundred of these sisters reclaimed from sin and death, through the efforts of one woman. She did what she could. What a grand harvest there will be, and how she will rejoice when she hears the Master say: "Well done, good and faithful servant."

I remember hearing of a man in one of the hospitals who received a bouquet of flowers from the Flower Mission. He looked at the beautiful bouquet and said: "Well, if I had known that a bunch of flowers could do a fellow so much good, I would have sent some myself when I was well." If people only knew how they might cheer some lonely heart and lift up some drooping spirit, or speak some word that shall be lasting in its effects for all coming time, they would be up and about it. If the Gospel is ever to be carried into the lanes and alleys, up to the attics and down into the cellars, we must all of us be about it. As I have said, if each of us will do what we can, a great multitude will be gathered into the kingdom of God.

Rev. Dr. Willets, of Philadelphia, in illustrating the blessedness of cultivating a liberal spirit, uses this beautiful figure—

"See that little fountain yonder—away yonder in the distant mountain, shining like a thread of silver through the thick copse, and sparkling like a diamond in its healthful activity. It is hurrying on with tinkling feet to bear its tribute to the river. See, it passes a stagnant pool, and the pool hails it: 'Whither away, master streamlet?' 'I am going to the river to bear this cup of water God has given me.' 'Ah, you are very foolish for that: you'll need it before the summer's over. It has been a backward spring, and we shall have a hot summer to pay for it—you will dry up then.' 'Well,' said the streamlet, 'if I am to die so soon, I had better work while the day lasts. If I am likely to lose this treasure from the heat, I had better do good with it while I have it.' So on it went, blessing and rejoicing in its course. The pool smiled complacently at its own superior foresight, and husbanded all its resources, letting not a drop steal away.

Soon the midsummer heat came down, and it fell upon the little stream. But the trees crowded to its brink, and threw out their sheltering branches over it in the day of adversity, for it brought refreshment and life to them, and the sun peeped through the branches and smiled complacently upon its dimpled face, and seemed to say, 'It's not in my heart to harm you;' and the birds sipped the silver tide, and sung its praises; the flowers breathed their perfume upon its bosom; the husbandman's eye always sparkled with joy, as he looked upon the line of verdant beauty that marked its course through his fields and meadows; and so on it went, blessing and blessed of all!

And where was the prudent pool? Alas! in its glorious inactivity it grew sickly and pestilential. The beasts of the field put their lips to it, but turned away without drinking; the breeze stopped and kissed it by mistake, but shrunk chilled away. It caught the malaria in the contact, and carried the ague through the region; the inhabitants caught it and had to move away; and at last, the very frogs cast their venom upon the pool and deserted it, and heaven, in mercy to man, smote it with a hotter breath and dried it up!

But did not the little stream exhaust itself? Oh, no? God saw to that. It emptied its full cup into the river, and the river bore it on to the sea, and the sea welcomed it, and the sun smiled upon the sea, and the sea sent up its incense to greet the sun, and the clouds caught in their capacious bosoms the incense from the sea, and the winds, like waiting steeds, caught the chariots of the clouds and bore them away—away to the very mountain that gave the little fountain birth, and there they tipped the brimming cup, and poured the grateful baptism down; and so God saw to it that the little fountain, though it gave so fully and so freely, never ran dry. And if God so blessed the fountain, will He not bless you, my friends, if, as ye have freely received, ye also freely give? Be assured He will."

A young lady belonging to a wealthy family in our country was sent to a fashionable boarding-school. In the school Christ had a true witness in one of the teachers. She was watching for an opportunity of reaching some of the pupils. When this young lady of wealth and position came, the teacher set her heart upon winning her to Christ. The first thing she did was to gain her affections. Let me say right here that we shall not do much toward reaching the people until we make them love us. This teacher, having won the heart of her pupil, began to talk to her about Christ, and she soon won her heart for the Savior. Then instead of dropping her as so many do, she began to show her the luxury of working for God. They worked together, and were successful in winning a good many of the young ladies in the school to Christ. When the pupil got a taste of work, that spoiled the world for her. Let me say to any Christian who is holding on to the world: Get into the Lord's work, and the world will soon leave you. You will not leave it, you will have something better. I pity those Christians who are all the time asking if they have to give up this thing and that thing. You won't be asking that when you get a taste of the Lord's work; you will then have something that the world cannot give you.

When this young lady went back to her home the parents were anxious that she should go out into worldly society. They gave a great many parties, but, to their great amazement, they could not get her interested. She was hungering for something else. She went to the Sabbath-school in connection with the church she attended, and asked the Superintendent to give her a class. He said there were really more teachers than he needed.

She tried for weeks to find something to do for Christ. One day as she was walking down the street, she saw a little boy coming out of a shoemaker's shop. The man had a wooden last in his hand, and he was running as fast as he could after the boy. When he found he could not overtake him, he hurled the last at him and hit him in the back. When the shoemaker had picked up his last and gone back to his shop, the boy stopped running and began to cry. The scene touched the heart of this young lady. When she got up to him she stopped and spoke to him kindly.

"Do you go to the Sabbath-school?" "No."

"Do you go to the day-school?" "No."

"What makes you cry?" He thought she was going to make sport of him, so he said it was none of her business. "But I am your friend," she said. He was not in the habit of having a young lady like that speak to him; at first he was afraid of her, but at last she won his confidence. Finally, she asked him to come to the Sabbath-school, and be in her class. No, he said, he didn't like study; he would not come. She said she would not ask him to study; she would tell him beautiful stories and there would be nice singing. At last he promised that he would come. He was to meet her on Sabbath morning, at the corner of a certain street.

She was not sure that he would keep his promise, but she was there at the appointed time, and he was there too. She took him to the school and said to the Superintendent: "Can you give me a place where I can teach this boy?" He had not combed his hair, and he was barefooted. They did not have any of that kind of children in the school, so the Superintendent looked at him, and said he did not know just where to put him. Finally he put him away in a corner, as far as he could from the others. There this young lady commenced her work — work that the angels would have been glad to do.

He went home and told his mother he thought he had been among the angels. When the mother found he was going to a Protestant school she told him he must not go again. When the father got to know it, he said he would flog him every time he went to the school. However, the boy went again the next Sabbath, and the father flogged him; every time he went he gave the poor boy a flogging. At last he said to his father: "I wish you would flog me before I go, and then I won't be thinking about it all the time I am at the school." You laugh at it, but, dear friends, let us remember that gentleness and love will break down the opposition in the hardest heart. These little diamonds will sparkle in the Savior's crown, if we will but search them out and polish them. We cannot make diamonds, but we can polish them if we will.

Finding that the flogging did not stop the boy from going to the school, the father said: "If you will give up the Sabbath-school, I will give you every Saturday afternoon to play, or you can have all you make by peddling." The boy went to his teacher and said: "I have been thinking that if you could meet me on the Saturday afternoon we would have longer time together than on the Sabbath." I wonder if there is a wealthy young lady reading this book who would give up her Saturday afternoons to teach a poor little boy the way into the kingdom of God. She said she would gladly do it; if any callers came she was always engaged on Saturdays. It was not long before the light broke into the darkened mind of the boy, and a change came into his life. She got him some good clothes and took an interest in him; she was a guardian angel to him. One day he was down at the railway station peddling. He was standing on the platform of the carriage, when the engine gave a sudden start; the little fellow was leaning on the edge, and his foot slipped so that he fell down and the train passed over his legs. When the doctor came, the first thing he said was: "Doctor, will I live to get home?" "No, my boy, you are dying." "Will you tell my father and mother that I died a Christian?" Did not the teacher get well paid for her work? She will be no stranger when she goes to the better land. That little boy will be waiting to give her a welcome.

It is a great thing to lead one soul from the darkness of sin into the glorious light of the Gospel. I believe if an angel were to wing his way from earth up to heaven, and were to say that there was one poor, ragged boy, without father or mother, with no one to care for him and teach him the way of life; and if God were to ask who among them was willing to come down to this earth and live here for fifty years and lead that one to Jesus Christ, every angel in heaven would volunteer to go. Even Gabriel, who stands in the presence of the Almighty, would say: "Let me leave my high and lofty position, and let me have the luxury of leading one soul to Jesus Christ." There is no greater honor than to be the instrument in God's hand of leading one person out of the kingdom of Satan into the glorious light of heaven.

I have this motto in my Bible, and I commend it to you: "Do all the good you can; to all the people you can; in all the ways you can; and as long as ever you can." If each of us will at once set about some work for God, and will keep at it 365 days in the year, then a good deal will be accomplished. Let us so live that it may be truthfully said of us: We have done what we could.

CHAPTER VIII

"WHO IS MY NEIGHBOR?"

You have no doubt frequently read the story of the good Samaritan. In this parable Christ brings before us four men. He draws the picture so vividly that the world will never forget it. Too often when we read the Scripture narratives they do not come home to our hearts, and it is not long before we forget the lesson that the Master would have us to learn and to remember.

We find that when Christ was on the earth there was a class of people who gathered round Him and were continually finding fault with everything He said and did. We read that on this occasion a lawyer came asking Him what he could do to inherit eternal life. Our Lord told him to keep the commandments—to love the Lord with all his heart, and his neighbor as himself. The lawyer then wanted to know who was his neighbor. In this narrative Christ told him who his neighbor was, and what it was to love him.

It seems to me that we have been a long while in finding out who is our neighbor. I think in the parable of the good Samaritan Christ has taught us very clearly that any man or woman who is in need of our love and our help—whether temporal or spiritual—is our neighbor. If we can render them any service we are to do it in the name of our Master.

Here we have brought before us two men, each of whom passed by one who was in great need—one who had fallen among the thieves, who had been stripped, wounded, and left there to die. The first that came down that road from Jerusalem to Jericho was a priest. As he went along the highway he heard a cry of distress, and he looked to see who was the unfortunate man. He could see that the poor sufferer was a Jew; it may be that he had seen him in the temple on the Sabbath day. But then he was not in his own parish now. His work was in the temple, and it was over for the present. He was a professional man, and he had gone through all that was required of him.

He was in a great hurry to get down to Jericho. It may be they were going to open a new synagogue there, and he was to dedicate it. A very important business, and of course he could not stop to help this poor, wounded, fallen man. So he passed on. It may be, as he went along, he reasoned with himself somewhat in this way: "I wonder why God ever permitted sin to enter the world at all. It is very strange that man should be in this fallen state." Or his thoughts may have taken another turn, and he said to himself that when he got down to Jericho he would form a committee to look after these unfortunate brethren. He would give something toward the expenses. Or he would try and get a policeman to go and look after those thieves who had stripped him.

He did not think that all the while this poor wounded man was dying. Most likely he was now crying for water, and it might be that there was a brook running by, within a few rods of the spot where he lay. Yet this priest never stopped to give him a drink. All his religion was in his head: it had never reached his heart. The one thought in his mind was duty, duty; and when he had got through that which he considered his duty, he fancied his work was done. God wants heart service; if we do not give Him that, we can render to Him no service at all.

We read that a Levite next came along the highway where this wounded man was lying in his helplessness. As he passed along he also heard the man's cry of distress. He turned aside for a moment to look at the poor fellow, and he could see that he was a son of Abraham—a brother Jew. But he also must hasten on to Jericho. Possibly he had to help in the ceremony of opening the new synagogue. Perhaps there was going to be a convention down there, on "How to reach the masses," and he was going to help discuss the point. I have noticed that many men now-a-days will go to a conference and talk for hours on that subject, but they will not themselves lift a hand to reach the masses.

The Levite's thoughts probably took another turn, and he said to himself: "I will see if I can't get a bill through the Legislature to prevent those thieves from robbing and wounding people." There are some now who think they can legislate men back to God—that they can prevent sin by legislation. Like the priest, this Levite never stopped to give the poor fellow a drop of water to quench his thirst; he never attempted to bind up his wounds or to help him in any way. He passed along the highway, doubtless, saying to himself, "I pity that poor fellow." There is a good deal of that kind of pity now-a-days; but it comes only from the lips, not from the heart.

The next one to come along that road was a Samaritan. Now it was notorious that in those days a Jew would not speak to a Samaritan; the very presence of the latter was pollution to an orthodox Jew. No Jew ever entered the habitation of the hated Samaritan; he would not eat at his table or drink from his well. Neither would he allow a Samaritan to come under his roof. No religious Jew would even buy from a Samaritan, or sell to him. You know a Jew must have a very poor opinion of a man if he will not do business with him, when there is a prospect of making something out of him.

Not only was this the case, but the Jews considered that the Samaritans had no souls; that when they died they would be annihilated. Their graves would be so deep that not even the sound of Gabriel's trump would wake them on the resurrection morning. He was the only man under heaven who could not become a proselyte to the Jewish faith, and become a member of the Jewish family. Repentance was denied him in this life and the life to come. He might profess the Jewish religion; they would have nothing to do with him. That was the way in which they looked upon these men; yet Christ used the despised Samaritan to teach these bitter Jews the lesson of love to their neighbor.

The Samaritan came that way. It says in the narrative that the priest came down that way "by chance;" but we are not told that the Samaritan came by chance. He represents our Lord and Master. We are told that he came to where the poor wounded man was; he got off the beast on which he was riding and stooped right down there by the side of the sick man. He looked at him and saw that he was a Jew. If he had been like the Jews themselves, he would most likely have said, "Serve you right. I only wish the thieves had killed you outright. I would not lift a finger to help you, you poor wretched Samaritan." But no! not a word of condemnation or blame did he utter.

Let us learn a lesson from this. Do you think these drunkards need any one to condemn them? There is no one in the wide world who can condemn them as they condemn themselves. What they need is sympathy—tenderness, gentleness and kindness. This Samaritan did not pull a manuscript out of his pocket, and begin to read a long sermon to the wounded man. Some people seem to think that all the world needs is a lot of sermons. Why, the people of this land have been almost preached to death. What we want is to preach more sermons with our hands and feet—to carry the Gospel to the people by acts of kindness.

Neither did he read this poor Jew a long lecture, endeavoring to prove that science was better than religion. He did not give him a long address on geology; what could that do for him? What the poor man needed was sympathy and help. So the first thing the good Samaritan did was to pour oil into his wounds. How many wounded men there are in our midst who have need of the oil of pity and sympathy. A good many Christians seem always to carry about with them a bottle of vinegar, which they bring out on all occasions.

The Samaritan might have said to the man: "Why did you not stay at Jerusalem? What business had you to come down this road, any way, giving all this trouble?" So people will sometimes say to a young man who has come to the city and got into trouble: "Why did you ever leave your home and come to this wicked city?" They begin to scold and upbraid. You are never going to reach men and do them good in that way; or by putting yourself on a high platform; you have to come down to them and enter into their sorrows and troubles. See how this Samaritan "came to where he was," and instead of lecturing him, poured the healing oil into his wounds.

You observe there are twelve things mentioned in the narrative that the Samaritan did. We can dismiss in a word all that the priest and the Levite did — they did nothing.

(1.) He "came to where he was."

(2.) He "saw him;" he did not, like the priest, pass by on the other side.

(3.) He "had compassion on him." If we would be successful winners of souls we, too, must be moved with compassion for the lost and the perishing. We must sympathize with men in their sorrows and troubles, if we would hope to gain their affections and to do them good.

(4.) He "went to him." The Levite went toward him, but we are told that he, as well as the priest, "passed by on the other side."

(5.) He "bound up his wounds." Perhaps he had to tear up his own garments in order to bind them up.

(6.) He poured in oil and gave some wine to the fainting man.

(7.) He "set him on his own beast." Do you not think that this poor Jew must have looked with gratitude and tenderness on the Samaritan, as he was placed on the beast, while his deliverer walked by his side? All the prejudice in his heart must have disappeared long before they got to the end of their journey.

(8.) He "brought him to an inn."

(9.) He "took care of him." I was greatly touched at hearing of a Christian worker in one of the districts in London where we were, who met with a drinking man at the meeting. He saw that the man was in drink, so he took him home and stayed all night with him; then, when he got sober the next morning, he talked with him. Many are willing enough to talk with drunkards when they are sober, but how few there are who will go and hunt them up when they are in their fallen condition, and stay with them till they can be reasoned with about their salvation.

(10.) When he departed on the morrow, the good Samaritan asked the host to care for him.

(11.) He gave him some money to pay the bill.

(12.) He said: "Whatever thou spendest more, when I come again I will repay thee."

There is nothing I think in all the teachings of Christ that brings out the whole Gospel better than this parable. It is a perfect picture of Christ coming down to this world to seek and save the lost.

(1.) He came to this world of sin and sorrow where we were, laying by His glory for the time, that He might assume our human nature, and put Himself on a level with those He came to save.

(2.) He mingled with the poor and needy so that He might see their condition.

(3.) He was "moved with compassion" for the multitudes; how often this is recorded in the Gospels. We are told, on more than one occasion, that He wept as He thought of all the woe and distress that sin had brought upon the human family.

(4.) Wherever Jesus Christ heard of a case of sorrow or need He went at once. No cry of distress ever reached His ears in vain.

(5.) On one occasion He read from the prophets concerning Himself, "The Spirit of the Lord is upon me . . . . because the Lord hath . . . . sent me to bind up the broken-hearted." He Himself was wounded, that the wounds which sin had made in us might be bound up and healed.

(6.) He not only comforted the sorrowing, but gave the promise of the Holy Spirit, Who was to bring comfort and strength to His redeemed people.

(7.) As the good Samaritan set the wounded man on his own beast, so the Savior gives us the unfailing promise of His word on which we may rest during our pilgrim journey. He Himself has promised to be with us in spirit by the way.

(8.) He brings us to the place of rest—rest in His love, in His willingness to save, in His power to keep. At the last He will bring us to the home of everlasting rest.

(9.) When He was on the earth He took a personal interest in all that concerned His disciples, and

(10.) When He had gone up on high He sent another Comforter who should abide with the Church.

(11.) He has furnished the Church with all that is needful for her support and growth in grace.

(12.) He will come again and reward His servants for all their faithful service.

Do you want to know how you can reach the masses? Go to their homes and enter into sympathy with them; tell them you have come to do them good, and let them see that you have a heart to feel for them. When they find out that you really love them, all those things that are in their hearts against God and against

Christianity will be swept out of the way. Atheists may tell them that you only want to get their money, and that you do not really care for their happiness. We have to contradict that lie by our lives, and send it back to the pit where it came from.

We are not going to do it unless we go personally to them and prove that we really love them. There are hundreds and thousands of families that could easily be reached if we had thousands of Christians going to them and entering into sympathy with their sorrows. That is what they want. This poor world is groaning and sighing for sympathy—human sympathy. I am quite sure it was that in Christ's life which touched the hearts of the common people. He made Himself one with them. He who was rich for our sakes became poor. He was born in the manger so that He might put himself on a level with the lowest of the low.

I think that in this matter He teaches His disciples a lesson. He wants us to convince the world that He is their friend. They do not believe it. If once the world were to grasp this thought, that Jesus Christ is the Friend of the sinner, they would soon flock to Him. I am sure that ninety-nine in every hundred of those out of Christ think that, instead of loving them, God hates them. How are they to find out their mistake? They do not attend our churches; and if they did there are many places where they would not hear it. Do you think that if those poor harlots walking the streets of our cities really believed that Jesus Christ loved them and wanted to be their friend—that if He were here in person He would not condemn them, but would take sides with them, and try to lift them up—they would go on in their sins? Do you think the poor drunkard who reels along the street really believes that Christ is his friend and loves him? The Scripture plainly teaches that though Christ hates sin He loves the sinner. This story of the good Samaritan is given to teach us this lesson. Let us publish abroad the good news that Christ loves sinners, and came into the world that He might save them.

There was a man who lived in one of our large cities. He died quite suddenly, and it was not long before his wife followed him to the grave. They left two boys, and there was a wealthy citizen who took the more promising of the boys and adopted him. The other boy was placed in the orphan asylum. He had never been away from his father and mother during their lives, and he had not been separated from his brother before. Every night he would go to sleep crying for his brother. One night they could not find him. Next morning he was found under the steps of the house of the wealthy banker who had adopted his little brother. When they asked him why he had left a good comfortable bed at the orphan home and stayed out there all night in the cold, he said he wanted to get near Charlie. He knew that if he rang the bell and they found him at the door they would send him hack, and it was a comfort to him to be near Charlie, even if he had to pass the night out there. His young heart was craving for sympathy, and he knew that Charlie loved him as no one else in the world did. If we can only convince these poor lost ones that some one loves them, then their hearts will be moved.

During the war a little boy, Frankie Bragg, was placed in one of the hospitals. He said it was so hard to be there away from all those who loved him. The nurse who was attending him, bent down and kissed him, and said she loved him. "Do you love me?" he said; "kiss me again; that was like my sister's kiss?" The nurse kissed him again, and he said with a smile: "It is not hard for me to die now, when I know that some one loves me." If we had more of this sympathy for the lost and the sorrowing, the world would soon feel our influence.

Shall we not learn a lesson from the good Samaritan? Let us hear the voice of the Master saying: "Go thou and do likewise." We can all do something. If we cannot reach the older people, let us try and win the young. It is a blessed privilege to be used of God to bring one little lamb into the kingdom. If we are only the means of saving one child our life will not be a failure; we shall hear the Master's "Well done, good and faithful servant."

A lady started a hospital for sick crippled children in Edinburgh two years ago. I was asking her if she had been blessed in the work. I shall not forget how her face lit up. She was in one of our recent meetings in London, and her face was beaming. She was telling of some very interesting cases of conversion among the children. What a privilege it is to lead these afflicted ones into the kingdom of God.

A little boy was brought to Edinburgh from Fife. There was no room in the children's hospital, and he was taken to the general hospital. He was only six years old; his father was dead; his mother was sick, so that she could not take care of him, and he had to be brought to the hospital in Edinburgh. My friend, Rev. George Wilson, went in one day and sat at the bedside of the little sufferer. He was telling him that the doctor was coming on Thursday to take off his little leg. You parents can imagine, if one of your children, six years old, away from home, and in a hospital, were told that the doctor was coming on a certain day to take his leg off, how he would suffer at the thought. The little fellow, of course, was in great trouble about it. The minister wanted to know about his mother; she was sick and his father was dead. The minister wished to comfort him, and he said: "The nurse is such a good woman; she will help you." "Yes," said the boy, "and perhaps Jesus will be with me." Do you have any doubt of it? Next Friday the man of God went to the hospital, but he found the cot was empty. The poor boy was gone; the Savior had come and taken him to His bosom.

In our great cities are there not hundreds and thousands who are in some need of human sympathy? That will speak to their hearts a good deal louder than eloquent sermons. Many will not be moved by eloquent sermons, who would yield to tenderness and gentleness and sympathy.

Said the great Dr. Chalmers: "The little that I have seen in the world, and know of the history of mankind, teaches me to look upon their errors in sorrow, not in anger. When I take the one poor heart that has sinned and suffered, and represent to myself the struggles and temptations it has passed through; the brief pulsation of joy; the tears of regret; the feebleness of purpose; the scorn of the world that has little charity; the desolation of the soul's sanctuary and threatening voices within; health gone—happiness gone—I would fain leave the erring soul of my fellowman with Him from whose hands it came."

Some of you may say: "How am I to get into sympathy with those who are in sorrow?" That is a very important question. Many people go to work for God, but they seem to do it in such a professional way. I will tell you how you can be brought into sympathy. I have found this rule to be of great help to me. Put yourself in the place of the sorrowing and afflicted ones, with whom you want to sympathize. If you do that you will soon gain their affections and be able to help them.

God taught me a lesson a few years ago that I shall never forget. I was Superintendent of a Sunday-school in Chicago with over 1,500 scholars. In the months of July and August many deaths took place among the children, and as most of the ministers were out of the city I had to attend a great many funerals. Sometimes I had to be at four or five in one day. I was so accustomed to it that I got to do it almost mechanically. I could see the mother take her last look at the child, and see the coffin lid closed without being moved by it.

One day when I came home my wife told me that one of the Sunday-school children had been drowned, and the mother wanted to see me. I took my little daughter with me and we went to the house. I found the father in one corner of the room drunk. The mother told me that she took in washing in order to get a living for herself and her children, as her husband drank up all his wages. Little Adelaide used to go to the river and gather the floating wood for the fire. That day she had gone as usual; she saw a piece of wood out a little way from the bank; in stretching out to reach it she slipped, and fell into the water and was drowned. The mother told me her sad story; how she had no money to buy the shroud and the coffin, and she wanted me to help her. I took out my note-book and put down her name and address, and took the measure of the coffin, in order to send it to the undertakers.

The poor mother was much distressed, but it did not seem to move me. I told her I would be at the funeral, and then I left. As my little girl walked by my side she said to me: "Papa, suppose we were very poor, and mamma had to wash for a living, and I had to go to the river to get sticks to make a fire; if I were to fall into the water and get drowned would you feel bad?" "Feel bad! Why, my child, I do not know what I should do. You are my only daughter, and if you were taken from me I think it would break my heart." And I took her to my bosom and kissed her. "Then did you feel bad for that mother?" How that question cut me to the heart.

I went back to the house, and took out my Bible and read to the mother the fourteenth chapter of John. Then I prayed with her and endeavored to comfort her. When the day for the funeral arrived I attended it. I had not been to the cemetery for a good many years; I had thought my time was too precious, as it was some miles away. I found the father was still drunk. I had got a lot in the strangers' field for little Adelaide. As we were laying the coffin in the grave another funeral procession came up, and the corpse was going to be laid near by. Adelaide's mother said, as we were covering up the coffin: "Mr. Moody, it is very hard to lay her away among strangers. I have been moving about a good deal, and have lived among strangers, and I have never had a burying-lot. It is very hard to place my firstborn among strangers." I said to myself that it would be pretty hard to have to bury my child in the strangers' field. I had got into full sympathy with the poor mother by this time.

Next Sabbath I told the children in the Sunday-school what had taken place. I suggested that we should buy a Sunday-school lot, and when any of the children attending the school died, they would not be laid in the strangers' field, but would be put in our own lot. Before we could get the title made out, a mother came and wanted to know if her little girl who had just died could be buried in the lot. I told her I would give permission. I went to the funeral, and as we were lowering the little coffin I asked what was the name. She said it was Emma. That was the name of my own little girl, and I could not help but weep as I thought of how I would feel if it were my own Emma. Do you tell me I could not sympathize with that bereaved mother? Very soon afterward, another mother came and wished to have her dead child buried in our lot. She told me his name was Willie. At that time that was the name of my only boy, and I thought how it would be with me if it were my Willie who was dead. So the first children buried there bore the names of my two children. I tried to put myself in the places of these sorrowing mothers, and then it was easy for me to sympathize with them in their grief, and point them to Him who "shall wipe away all tears from their eyes."

About the first thing I did when I returned to Chicago nine years ago, was to drive up to and see our children's lot. I thought it would last a good many years, but it was about full, for many of my old Sabbath-school scholars had gone while I had been away, and their bodies were resting in this lot till the great day. I understood, however, that the children of the Sabbath-school were about to purchase another and a larger lot which would suffice for many years under ordinary circumstances. Many little ones are laid there, waiting for the resurrection, and I would like to be buried beside them, it would be so sweet to be in their company when we rise and meet our Lord.

Dear friends, if you would get into full sympathy with others put yourself in their places. May God fill our hearts with the spirit of the good Samaritan, so that we may be filled with tenderness and love and compassion.

I want to give you a motto that has been a great help to me. It was a Quaker's motto:

"I expect to pass through this world but once. If, therefore, if there be any kindness I can show or any good thing I can do to any fellow human being let me do it now; let me not defer nor neglect it, for I will not pass this way again."

CHAPTER IX

"YE ARE THE LIGHT OF THE WORLD"

"They that be wise shall shine as the brightness of the firmament; and they that turn many to righteousness as the stars for ever and ever."

That is the testimony of an old man, and one who had the richest and deepest experience of any man living on the face of the earth at the time. He was taken down to Babylon when a young man; some Bible students think he was not more than twenty years of age. If any one had said, when this young Hebrew was carried away into captivity, that he would outrank all the mighty men of that day—that all the generals who had been victorious in almost every nation at that time were going to be eclipsed by this young slave—probably no one would have believed it. Yet for five hundred years no man whose life is recorded in history shone as did this man. He outshone Nebuchadnezzar, Belshazzar, Cyrus, Darius, and all the princes and mighty monarchs of his day.

We are not told when he was converted to a knowledge of the true God, but I think we have good reason to believe that he had been brought under the influence of Jeremiah the prophet. Evidently some earnest, Godly man, and no worldly professor, had made a deep impression upon him. Some had at any rate taught him how he was to serve God.

We hear people nowadays talking about the hardness of the field where they labor; they say their position is a very peculiar one. Think of the field in which Daniel had to work. He was not only a slave, but he was held captive by a nation that detested the Hebrews. The language was unknown to him. There he was among idolaters; yet he commenced at once to shine. He took his stand for God from the very first, and so he went on through his whole life. He gave the dew of his youth to God, and he continued faithful right on till his pilgrimage was ended.

Notice that all those who have made a deep impression on the world, and have shone most brightly, have been men who lived in a dark day. Look at Joseph; he was sold as a slave into Egypt by the Ishmaelites; yet he took his God with him into captivity, as Daniel afterward did. And he remained true to the last; he did not give up his faith because he had been taken away from home and placed among idolaters. He stood firm, and God stood by him.

Look at Moses, who turned his back upon the gilded palaces of Egypt, and identified himself with his despised and down-trodden nation. If a man ever had a hard field it was Moses; yet he shone brightly, and never proved unfaithful to his God.

Elijah lived in a far darker day than we do. The whole nation was going over to idolatry. Ahab, and his queen, and all the royal court were throwing their influence against the worship of the true God. Yet Elijah stood firm, and shone brightly in that dark and evil day. How his name stands out on the page of history!

Look at John the Baptist. I used to think I would like to live in the days of the prophets; but I have given up that idea. You may be sure that when a prophet appears on the scene, everything is dark, and the professing Church of God has gone over to the service of the god of this world. So it was when John the Baptist made his appearance. See how his name shines out to-day! Eighteen centuries have rolled away, and yet the fame of that wilderness preacher shines brighter than ever. He was looked down upon in his day and generation, but he has outlived all his enemies; his name will be reverenced and his work remembered as long as the Church is on the earth.

Talk about your field being a hard one! See how Paul shone for God as he went out, the first missionary to the heathen, telling them of the God whom he served, and Who had sent His Son to die a cruel death in order to save the world. Men reviled him and his teachings; they laughed him to scorn when he spoke of the Crucified One. But he went on preaching the Gospel of the Son of God. He was regarded as a poor tent-maker by the great and mighty ones of his day; but no one can now tell the name of any of his persecutors, or of those who lived at that time, unless their names happen to be associated with his, and they were brought into contact with him.

Now the fact is, all men like to shine. We may as well acknowledge it at once. You go into business circles and see how men struggle to get into the front rank. Every one wants to outshine his neighbor and to stand at the head of his profession. Go into the political world and see how there is a struggle going on as to who shall be the greatest. If you go into a school you find that there is a rivalry among the boys and girls. They all want to stand at the top of the class. When a boy does reach this position and outranks all the rest the mother is very proud of it. She will manage to tell all the neighbors how Johnnie has got on, and what a number of prizes he has gained.

You go into the army and you find the same thing—one trying to outstrip the other; every one is very anxious to shine and rise above his comrades. Go among the young men in their games and see how anxious the one is to outdo the other. So we have all that desire in us; we like to shine above our fellows.

And yet there are very few who can really shine in the world. Once in a while one man will outstrip all his competitors. Every four years what a struggle goes on throughout our country as to who shall be the President of the United States, the battle raging for six months or a year. Yet only one man can get the prize. There a good many struggling to get the place, but many are disappointed, because only one can attain the coveted prize. But in the kingdom of God the very least and the very weakest may shine if they will. Not only can one obtain the prize, but all may have it if they will.

It does not say in this passage that the Statesmen are going to shine as the brightness of the firmament. The Statesmen of Babylon are gone; their very names are forgotten.

It does not say that the nobility are going to shine. Earth's nobility are soon forgotten. John Bunyan, the Bedford tinker, has outlived the whole crowd of those who were the nobility in his day. They lived for self, and their memory is blotted out. He lived for God and for souls, and his name is as fragrant as ever it was.

We are not told that the merchants are going to shine. Who can tell the name of any of the millionaires of Daniel's day? They were all buried in oblivion a few years after their death. Who were the mighty conquerors of that day? But few can tell. It is true that we hear of Nebuchadnezzar, but probably we should not have known very much about him but for his relations to the prophet Daniel.

How different with this faithful prophet of the Lord. Twenty-five centuries have passed away, and his name shines on, and on, and on, brighter and brighter. And it is going to shine while the Church of God exists. "They that be wise shall shine as the brightness of the firmament; and they that turn many to righteousness as the stars for ever and ever."

How quickly the glory of this world fades away! Seventy-five years ago the great Napoleon almost made the earth to tremble. How he blazed and shone as an earthly warrior for a little while! A few years passed, and a little island held that once proud and mighty conqueror; he died as a poor broken-hearted prisoner. Where is he to-day? Almost forgotten. Who in all the world will say that Napoleon lives in their heart's affections?

But look at this despised and hated Hebrew prophet. They wanted to put him into the lions' den because he was too sanctimonious and too religious. Yet see how green his memory is to-day! How his name is loved and honored for his faithfulness to his God.

Seventeen years ago I was in Paris at the time of the Great Exhibition. Napoleon the Third was then in his glory. Cheer after cheer would rise up as he drove along the streets of the city. A few short years and he fell from his lofty estate. He died an exile from his country and his throne, and where is his name today? Very few think about him at all, and if his name is mentioned it is not with love and esteem. How empty and short-lived are the glory and the pride of this world! if we are wise we will live for God and eternity; we will get outside of ourselves, and will care nothing for the honor and glory of this world.

In Proverbs we read: "He that winneth souls is wise." If any man, woman, or child by a Godly life and example can win one soul to God, their life will not have been a failure. They will have outshone all the mighty men of their day, because they will have set a stream in motion that will flow on and on for ever and ever. That little boy may shine in God's kingdom if he will.

God has left us down here to shine. We are not here to buy and sell and get gain, to accumulate wealth, to acquire worldly position. This earth, if we are Christians, is not our home; it is up yonder. God has sent us into the world to shine for Him—to light up this dark world. Christ came to be the Light of the world, but men put out that light. They took it to Calvary and blew it out. Before Christ went up on high He said to His disciples: "Ye are the light of the world. Ye are my witnesses. Go forth and carry the Gospel to the perishing nations of the earth."

So God has called us to shine, just as much as Daniel was sent into Babylon to shine. Let no man of woman say that they cannot shine because they have not so much influence as some others may have. What God wants you to do is to use the influence you have. Daniel probably did not have much influence down in Babylon at first, but God soon gave him more, because he was faithful and used what he had.

Remember a small light will do a good deal when it is in a very dark place. You put one little tallow candle in the middle of a large hall, and it will give a good deal of light.

Away out in the prairie regions, when meetings are held at night in the log school-houses, the announcement of the meeting is given out in this way: "A meeting will be held by early candle-light." The first man who comes brings a tallow-dip with him. It is perhaps all he has; but he brings it and sets it on the desk. It does not light the building much; but it is better than none at all. The next man brings his candle; and the next family bring their candles. By the time the house is full, there is plenty of light. So if we all shine a little, there will be a good deal of light. That is what God wants us to do. If we cannot all be lighthouses, any one of us can at any rate be a tallow candle.

A little light will sometimes do a great deal. The city of Chicago was set on fire by a cow kicking over a lamp, and a hundred thousand people were burnt out of house and home. Do not let Satan get the advantage of you, and make you think that because you cannot do any great thing you cannot do anything at all.

Then we must remember that we are to let our light shine. It does not say, "Make your light shine." You do not have to make light to shine; all you have to do is to let it shine.

I remember hearing of a man at sea who was very sea-sick. If there is a time when a man feels that he cannot do any work for the Lord it is then—in my opinion. While this man was sick he heard that a man had fallen overboard. He was wondering if he could do anything to help to save the man. He laid hold of a light and held it up to the port-hole. The drowning man was saved. When this man got over his attack of sickness he got up on deck one day, and was talking with the man who was rescued. The saved man gave this testimony. He said he had gone down the second time, and was just going down again for the last time, when he put out his hand. Just then, he said, some one held a light at the port-hole, and the light fell on his hand. A man caught him by the hand and pulled him into the lifeboat.

It seemed a small thing to do to hold up the light; yet it saved the man's life. If you cannot do some great thing you can hold the light for some poor, perishing drunkard, who may be won to Christ and delivered from destruction. Let us take the torch of salvation and go into these dark homes, and hold up Christ to the people as the Savior of the world. If these perishing masses are to be reached we must lay our lives right alongside theirs, and pray with them and labor for them. I would not give much for a man's Christianity, if he is saved himself and is not willing to try and save others. It seems to me the basest ingratitude if we do not reach out the hand to others who are down in the same pit from which we were delivered. Who is able to reach and help these drinking men like those who have themselves been slaves to the intoxicating cup? Will you not go out this very day and seek to rescue these men? If we were all to do what we can we should soon empty the drinking saloons.

I remember reading of a blind man who was found sitting at the corner of a street in a great city with a lantern beside him. Some one went up to him and asked what he had the lantern there for, seeing that he was blind, and the light was the same to him as the darkness. The blind man replied: "I have it so that no one may stumble over me."

Dear friends, let us think of that. Where one man reads the Bible, a hundred read you and me. That is what Paul meant when he said we were to be living epistles of Christ, known and read of all men. I would not give much for all that can be done by sermons, if we do not preach Christ by our lives. If we do not commend the Gospel to people by our holy walk and conversation, we shall not win them to Christ. Some little act of kindness will perhaps do more to influence them than any number of long sermons.

A vessel was caught in a storm on Lake Erie, and they were trying to make for the harbor of Cleveland. At the entrance of that port they had what are called the upper lights and the lower lights. Away back on the bluffs were the upper lights burning brightly enough; but when they came near the harbor they could not see the lights showing the entrance to it. The pilot said he thought they had better get back on the lake again. The Captain said he was sure they would go down if they went back, and he urged the pilot to do what he could to gain the harbor. The pilot said there was very little hope of making for the harbor, as he had nothing to guide him as to how he should steer the ship. They tried all they could to get her into the harbor. She rode on the top of the waves, and then into the trough of the sea, and at last they found themselves stranded on the beach, where the vessel was dashed to pieces. Some one had neglected the lower lights and they had gone out.

Let us take warning. God keeps the upper lights burning as brightly as ever, but He has left us down here to keep the lower lights burning. We are to represent Him here, as Christ represents us up yonder. I sometimes think if we had as poor a representative in the courts above as God has down here on earth, we would have a pretty poor chance of heaven. Let us have our loins girt and our lights brightly burning, so that others may see the way and not walk in darkness.

In the book of Revelation we read: "Blessed are the dead which die in the Lord from henceforth: yea, saith the Spirit, that they may rest from their labors; and their works do follow them."

There are many mentioned in the Scriptures of whom we read that they lived so many years and then they died. The cradle and the grave are brought close together: they lived and they died, and that is all we know about them. So in these days you could write on the tombstone of a great many professing Christians that they were born on such a day and they died on such a day; there is nothing whatever between.

But there is one thing you cannot bury with a good man; his influence still lives. They have not buried Daniel yet; his influence is as great to-day as ever it was. Do you tell me that Joseph is dead? His influence still lives and will continue to live on and on. You may bury the frail tenement of clay that a good man lives in, but you cannot get rid of his influence and example. Paul was never more powerful than he is to-day.

Do you tell me that John Howard, who went into so many of the dark prisons in Europe, is dead? Is Henry Martyn, or Wilberforce, or John Bunyan dead? Go into the Southern States and there you will find from three to four millions of men and women who once were slaves. You mention to any of them the name of Wilberforce, and see how quickly the eye will light up. He lived for something else besides himself, and his memory will never die out of the hearts of those for whom he lived and labored.

Is Wesley or Whitefield dead? The names of those great evangelists were never more honored than they are now. Is John Knox dead? You can go to any part of Scotland to-day and you will feel the power of his influence.

I will not tell you who are dead. The enemies of these servants of God—those who persecuted them and told lies about them. But the men themselves have outlived all the lies that were uttered concerning them. Not only that; they will shine in another world. How true are the words of the old Book: "They that be wise shall shine as the brightness of the firmament; and they that turn many to righteousness as the stars for ever and ever."

Let us go on turning as many as we can to righteousness. Let us be dead to the world, to its lies, its pleasures, and its ambitions. Let us live for God, continually going forth to win souls for Him.

Let me quote a few words by Dr. Chalmers. "Thousands of men breathe, move and live, pass off the stage of life, and are heard of no more—Why? They do not partake of good in the world, and none were blessed by them; none could point to them as the means of their redemption; not a line they wrote, not a word they spoke could be recalled; and so they perished; their light went out in darkness, and they were not remembered more than insects of yesterday. Will you thus live and die, O man immortal? Live for something. Do good, and leave behind you a monument of virtue that the storm of time can never destroy. Write your name in kindness, love and mercy, on the hearts of the thousands you come in contact with year by year; you will never be forgotten. No, your name, your deeds will be as legible on the hearts you leave behind as the stars on the brow of evening. Good deeds will shine as the stars of heaven."

www.ingramcontent.com/pod-product-compliance
Lightning Source LLC
Chambersburg PA
CBHW011803040426
42450CB00017B/3453